T0367604

God is Love

William Sutherland

Dedicated to God for His *agape* love towards all creation so that all may know God's true nature. He is all things of which love is the greatest.

Order this book online at www.trafford.com
or email orders@trafford.com

Most Trafford titles are also available at major online book retailers.

© Copyright 2013 William Sutherland.
All rights reserved. No part of this publication may be reproduced, stored in a retrieval system, or transmitted, in any form or by any means, electronic, mechanical, photocopying, recording, or otherwise, without the written prior permission of the author.

Cover: Merged Images from Shutterstock consisting of Open Heart symbolizing God's everlasting outpouring of love, Scriptural Text and depiction of a Crown of Thorns worn by the Universal Savior during his crucifixion.

Printed in the United States of America.

ISBN: 978-1-4907-1243-7 (sc)
ISBN: 978-1-4907-1245-1 (hc)
ISBN: 978-1-4907-1244-4 (e)

Library of Congress Control Number: 2013915140

Trafford rev. 10/22/2013

 www.trafford.com

North America & international
toll-free: 1 888 232 4444 (USA & Canada)
fax: 812 355 4082

Contents

Prologue

"There is no fear in love, but perfect love casts out fear. For fear has to do with punishment, and whoever fears has not been perfected in love.
[1 John 4:18]

Love is not about fear and is not gained or spread through coercion, duress or intimidation. In fact, fear and threats of punishment can never be a part of any loving relationship since they constitute elements of abuse. Because of this, one should not feel compelled to act in a certain way (e.g. fulfillment of the golden rule, ten commandments and/or two great commandments) or reciprocate God's love to the Creator Himself and His creation out of fear. Rather, one should make a sincere effort to uphold God's commandments and reciprocate His *agape* love out of free will, a desire to do so, gratitude, and love.

With that said, there should be no reason to fear God. Instead one should be in awe of God and not for the reasons so commonly and mistakenly cited – power, might and His all-knowing nature or because of the threat of divine punishment because of erroneous views that describe it as intensely painful and possibly eternal. Rest assured, God only punishes out of love such that divine punishment is for our own good and finite and

i

redemptive in nature. Though divine punishment may be unpleasant, it is not torture and it certainly does not kill since God's love is life itself. Furthermore, as God's love is the utmost opposite of even the slightest hate, which kills and destroys – it can only preserve and heal!

Accordingly, we should be in awe of God merely because of His *agape* love – a love that is so generous it creates and sustains life, is so powerful it overcomes and transcends death, and is so redemptive it is the sole means of salvation for each and every being of creation. Based on these examples alone, God's love *is* His power and might! There is nothing greater or stronger and it cannot be limited or stopped!

It is for this reason, St. Thérèse of Lisieux (1873-1897) wrote, *"How can I fear a God Who is nothing but mercy and love."*[1]

God is love is written so that fear may be dispelled and all may discover and know God's perfect love for each of us, a love that bridges every generation, transcends all religions, and ultimately leads to universal salvation. It is a love so powerful, so inclusive, so unconditional and so merciful there is no reason for fear.

In addition, God's love is not confined by time or space nor restricted by natural or spiritual boundaries. It was and always will be. It is infinite and everywhere – in every creature and every universe in the natural realm and in heaven, purgatory and hell, depending on one's beliefs, in the spiritual realm.

May *God is love* through comparative theology inspire, increase our faith, help us to better appreciate our individual worth and facilitate harmony between peoples and religions.

The reason *God is Love* utilizes comparative theology is because God's love is too widespread and profound to be limited to a single religion or specific doctrine or set of dogma. In fact, if God's love was viewed in its totality, there would not be enough room in all the universes to profess and/or record everything!

Accordingly, since God's love is everywhere and in every religion, a greater understanding and appreciation of His love can only be attained through the use of quotes and scriptures from a diversity of religious sources. In addition, *God is Love,* at times also uses secular sources since God's love is also present in secular writings and the secular world. After all, it is everywhere and cannot be contained!

At the same time, God's love is also the greatest as was demonstrated through the Universal Savior – Jesus the Christ (c. 5 BCE-33 CE). Out of love, God provided universal salvation through Himself. It is because of this that even when the different religions appear to diverge greatly or do not overtly recognize the Universal Savior – Jesus through love provides their individual salvific grace. The same can even be said with regard to the theology of atheism. Though God is deliberately ignored in its literature as if He does not exist, the Universal Savior still provides salvation to atheists!

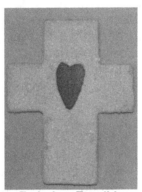

**Enduring, Tangible
Reminder of Divine Love**

The crucifixion and resurrection, all manifestations of God's *agape* love are that powerful! Thus, the cross serves as an enduring, tangible reminder of

Divine love for each and every one of us, past, present and future.

Because of this, no one – not even for a moment – should feel alienated let alone to such a degree that they sever ties with their Creator merely because of critical, condemning or biased scriptural writings, the acts or words of religious leaders, and/or policies and teachings of religious institutions.

If some person, scripture, religion and/or religious institution makes you feel rejected, that God does not love you, has abandoned you or will condemn you, do not despair. Their message is not of God nor an accurate reflection of His very being, which is unconditional, everlasting and most importantly, salvific love.

Thus, the intent of any religion must never be to exclude, divide, subvert or condemn. Instead it must be to include, unite, liberate, and above all, to love.

Why? Because anything that is of God reflects and upholds His love so that each being, regardless of physical, biological, ethnic and personal traits is drawn to Him. Everything that is of God makes one want to embrace and spread His love out of joy and gratitude!

Why? Because the natural, instinctive response to God's love is for the heart to leap with ecstatic joy since it has gotten a tiny taste of the imperishable bliss to come when we are reunited with the Creator in His kingdom of everlasting love.

Let all stand together and love one another and love and worship the one, only and same, living God to fulfill the Lord's loving desire *"that [all] may be one..."* [John 17:11]

It is for this reason, saints come from a diversity of theological backgrounds (e.g. Christian, Hindu, Sufi), mystics, who have had personal revelation and intimate contact with God have held a variety of faiths (e.g. Jewish, Christian, Islamic, Hindu), prophets can be counted from among the religions of East and West alike (e.g. Christian, Buddhist, Islamic) and God goes by many names.

Most of all, through *God is Love*, may each and every person who has been alienated from God return to and embrace His *agape* love and know there is nothing that can separate a single being of creation from this love – not a single person, not society, not a religious institution, and not even death!

Through unity found in the diversity of faiths, may we abstain from condemnation and live the prayer of St. Francis of Assisi (1181-1226 CE) as we strive to follow God's simple commandments that can be expressed in one word – *"Love."* [Galatians 5:14]

"Lord, make me an instrument of [Y]our peace. Where there is hatred, let me sow love..."

Let us then pray, "Lord, touch my heart with Your unconditional love and make it Your own so that I may love as You, free of preconceptions and subjective biases... Let me show love especially to those who are rejected and alienated."

At the same time, let the world's religions focus on God's love and unite to combat the afflictions that plague humanity – injustice, war, discrimination, disease, hunger, and poverty through demands for justice, conflict resolution, compassion, charity, respect, and promotion of scientific and intellectual research to truly fulfill God's loving desire for us on this earth.

When this is accomplished peace will have a much-needed chance to prevail and self-identity, scientific knowledge, political freedom, and religious pluralism will finally be respected and permitted to flourish. Difficult as this may seem, history has shown it is possible based on the examples of Cyrus the Great (576-530 BCE), the early Pauline church (c. 53-180 CE), and Mohammed (570-632 CE), the founder of Islam.

Under the rule of Cyrus the Great, the Achaemenid Empire was a blueprint for tolerance, cultural protection and human rights. There was no discrimination based on race, nationality, gender, age, and even sexual orientation. In fact, Cyrus the Great authored the world's first charter of human rights (the "Cyrus Cylinder") in 539 BCE that forbid class division or structure, considered all people to be equal, and guaranteed freedom of religion. It is because of this tolerance and foresight that religion and human rights, contrary to the opinion of some, are inextricably linked and interdependent.

Even though the relationship between religion and human rights can be complex and at times seemingly incompatible (e.g. when flawed edicts subvert human dignity and/or discriminate) both are not only compatible but also essential for the "cosmic order"[2] (predicated on good vs. evil as well as the concepts of yin and yang, and karma), universalist in nature (inalienable human rights apply to each and every person without exception and each religion ought lead to God's love and salvation), and demanding of social justice – The Immunity 9:71 *"[B]oth men and women, [ought be] friends and protectors of one another..."* [Islam]

"No one is superior or inferior..." [Hinduism: Rig
Veda 5:60:5]

*"Know ye not why [I] created you all from the same
dust? That no one should exalt himself over the
other."*[3] [Bahai'ism]

In reality, we are all born in the same way –
helpless without a single material possession to our
name – we enter eternity in the same way –
through corporeal death, in absolute need of God's
mercy without a single earthly possession to our
name. Why? Because God's love guarantees
equality both in this life and in eternity since He
cannot love a single member of His creation more
than another!

This is a good thing since each of us is spiritually
equal in that we are sinners far from perfection.
Accordingly we need God's love especially if we
are to have any chance for eternity. It is because
of this that God views each person as equally
priceless, equally worthy of respect and equally
deserving of His love.

Therefore, any form of discrimination or bigotry is
an affront to God since it contradicts His love and
mocks His judgment. It is as if we are saying – "We
know better, He is imperfect, He made a mistake
and His judgment and love are flawed!" Why?

Because God deliberately and lovingly planned and created the genetic code (DNA) that determines our self-identity. Therefore, if for example some race, gender or another trait were not good – He would not have made them possible through our genetic code since He is perfect and all He creates is good!

At the same time, it is because of human rights and tolerance that the three Abrahamic (Judaism, Christianity, and Islam) faiths even exist today. Had it not been for Cyrus the Great, Judaism would have likely been stamped out rendering the formation of its eventual future offshoots of Christianity and Islam significantly more difficult and unlikely.

Of course even without these offshoots, God would have still found a way to initiate His salvific plan of love in another way since He is after all, competent, all-powerful, and all-loving.

Furthermore, since Cyrus the Great upheld tolerance and human rights, two aspects of freedom that are demanded of by God's love, he is referred to as "God's anointed" in Isaiah 45:1 and remains a model for today's and future societies.

Cyrus the Great   **Cyrus Cylinder (Reverse Side)**
[Light of Persia]

With regard to the early Pauline church, its leaders and members generally lived in peace with their neighbors (Jews and pagans alike) during the era of *Pax Romana*. When evangelizing, their aim was not to forcefully impose their beliefs on others. It was to persuade them to accept Christ of their own free will. At the same time, members of the Pauline church did not deem it necessary to condemn persons who expressed different views and/or practiced different faiths even if they had declined to alter their thought processes and religious beliefs after evangelization attempts.

This is a timeless example that is relevant today and a model for all future ages. Evangelization must never revert to forced assimilation and the belief that a single or specific doctrine or dogma is the only path to God's love. Such an approach has nothing positive to offer – it is destructive and deadly (e.g. hundreds of millions have died in religious conflicts while countless others such as witches, scholars, and dissidents have been ruthlessly tortured during religious persecution – all actions that are infinitely contrary to God's love). There is no need for such an approach since it enslaves and violates individual conscience and turns people away from God's love. Besides, God's love is everywhere and the cross of the Universal Savior is redemptive for the atheist and every one else regardless of one's faith.

Mohammed (570-632 CE), the founder of Islam serves as a third example. Little known to many, Mohammed was also a strong believer in religious pluralism, tolerance, and diversity. Thus, when he built the first Islamic state in 622 CE he made it a point to guarantee equality and religious freedom in the Constitution of Medina so that diverse peoples – Muslim and non-Muslim could live in peace and interact freely, which included cultural exchanges and dissemination of ideas.

Under early Islamic rule, discourse and ideas were exchanged freely by intellectuals and religious leaders of the diverse faiths without a need to concern themselves about potential adverse consequences for expressing divergent views.

A degree of assimilation also occurred as the diverse cultures influenced each other, which is evident in archeological evidence. Christians began to write their texts in Arabic, Muslims adopted certain Christian imagery (e.g. grapevines growing from pots based on John 15:1 – *"I am the true vine"*) and created the "blue Qu'ran" written in gold leaf, silver, and ink on parchment colored with indigo (c. 900-950 CE in Tunisia) based on a c. 600 CE Byzantine "Illuminated" Bible that had been written with gold lettering on purple dyed parchment.

Likewise, Judaism and Christianity continued to flourish along with native languages and arts under early Islamic rule. Consequently, Judaic and Christian images were freely produced until the end of the 8th century CE when Islam's inclusive vision began to wane following the demise of the Umayyad dynasty (c. 750 CE).

In fact during this period, the Islamic empire even became a refuge for Christians persecuted by other Christians, namely Constantinople's leaders during the Iconoclastic Controversy (8th-9th century CE). What is even more remarkble about Islamic tolerance of that period is that Muslims harbored these Christians even though they agreed with Constantinople's view. As a result, Christalogical differences were respected and production and veneration of icons by those who dissented continued unimpeded in the Islamic empire despite Constantinople's prohibition of their use.

At the same time, Mohammed, like Jesus was a strong believer in forgiveness such that he forgave those who had plotted against him in Mecca when the City fell to his army and a woman who had attempted to poison him. Why? Because God's love does not condemn and never will condemn!

In the same spirit, Hinduism avoids doctrinal condemnation of others since upholding and spreading God's love through charity and tolerance is considered paramount to judging or being right.

"Let there be openess in your... hearts and minds..." [Hinduism: Rig Veda 10:191:4]

This is imperative since God's love does not desire that anyone be alienated, humiliated or brought to grief – *"Let nobody suffer from grief."* [Excerpt from holy prayer of Hindus]   Yet that is the result each time a person is rejected and/or condemned.

In fact, Divine love suffers every time a victim of rejection and/or condemnation becomes alienated from God. Think of the emotional suffering a loving parent goes through when a child rejects them. Multiply this pain by infinity (∞) and that is the pain

God feels each time a person rejects Him! Why? Because as the Creator, He is the Father of each and every living being and His love for each and every being of creation is unsurpassed.

One can also use another analogy. Every artist (e.g. painter, sculptor, etc.) is grieved when a piece of their work is vandalized or destroyed. God, as the Creator is the ultimate artist – having sculpted the universes out of nothing and living creation out of organic matter called dust. Thus when a person is persecuted, rejected, alienated, condemned, harmed (physically and/or emotionally) and/or killed, God is greatly grieved since such acts constitute vandalism or destruction of His beloved creation. It does not matter if the acts were committed by individuals, religious leaders, religious institutions and/or society in general. The pain God feels is infinitely great, because a piece of His own self has been forcibly torn from Him!

Yet when persons, religions and/or society condemn, this is often the result. Worse yet, in response to condemnation, the victim often loses focus of God's love, feels abandoned and ultimately turns away from God. In fact, many atheists cite scriptural hatred, theological condemnation, and religious hyprocrisy for their rejection of God.

William Sutherland

Fortunately for us, with regard to the above, even when this happens, God is the Protector of all souls. Therefore, even if the body is harmed emotionally and/or physically or destroyed, the soul survives. No person or entity, except God alone can kill or destroy a soul. However, since *"God is love"* [1 John 4:8 and 16], Who offers us an endless stream of mercy, He will never do so. Furthermore, He will not do so because such a course of action would violate His very nature and being. Thus, God protects, cherishes and loves each and every soul unconditionally and will continue to do so for all eternity.

Only when people and even religions truly recognize the attributes of God's love – diversity, equality, and inclusion – and drop their innate fears and impulsive rejection of that which is different will we become a better and more loving society. No person should be ostracized even if their individuality (which in and of itself is a gift from God) causes them to stand out from the homogenous majority and/or violates social expectations of conformity. They are not rejected by God and certainly should not be considered pariahs or outcastes by religious instititions, society and individuals.

With that said, the next time one encounters some one who is different – one should focus on God's

xvi

love, keep an open mind and seek to understand or at least respect that person so that we do not create unbridgeable barriers to acceptance and inclusion.

We must find it in ourselves to follow God's loving call to embrace our differences and reject homogeneity-based social systems that value sameness over everything else. We cannot allow tribalism and other conformity-based social systems to impede our interaction with and love for people who do not meet the standards of these systems.

We must accept and love the person who is different, for we are all brothers and sisters of the same divine Creator Who is even more diverse than the human race! For example, with regard to Christianity, God is in the form of a spirit (the Father), a human being (the Universal Savior), and tongues of fire or a dove (the Holy Spirit). In Hinduism, God is both male and female. Why? In reality, the attributes of God reflect every race, every gender, and every being! Otherwise God would not be complete.

With regard to humanity, we are all members of the same human race. In short, we are all branches on the same vine and no branch should be broken or trampled upon to give preferential treatment to another.

To put it another way, we are one and as one suffers, we all suffer and as one rejoices, we all rejoice.

After all, when different individuals and groups came to the Universal Savior be it a leper, one possessed or suffering from mental illness, a tax collector, a Roman centurion, a Samaritan, crowds seeking his word, a sinner, etc. not once did Jesus turn them away or deny their petition! He loved, healed, fed, and forgave! Why? Because to God, no one is unlovable!

We must follow this loving example! And when we do this, we will discover that we simply have no time for judging and condemning. We will also discover that we are a lot more similar with a lot more in common than our differences may imply.

However, for this to be accomplished, we must liberate ourselves from the bondage of dependence on, the perceived need to uphold, and conformity to human-established norms that stifle and crush individuality. We must free ourselves of the need to belong to a group or appease the prevailing view of a majority. With regard to the latter, such appeasement is nothing less than ungodly tyranny when it results in alienation and pain. Only when we liberate and free ourselves can we be the person God desires – creative, wise and loving – an active force for justice and positive change.

In addition, as an extension of this, we must think like God. When we do so, we will ensure our respect and concern for another is equal – regardless of individuality, nationality, race, gender, age, religion, and disability (if applicable) – and fundamentally based on God's *agape* love. If we do not, and allow these factors to influence how we feel about someone, then we do not truly love them and our professed "love" is shallow and insincere.

Although it is not often easy to exercise sincere true love and it may be uncomfortable to do so, we must try. Few things in life are easy and true freedom mandates that we liberate ourselves from our comfort zones. Let God's love be our guide and give us the courage to open our hearts and make this challenging, but rewarding journey of love.

And when we stumble and fall, let our missteps inspire us so that we have the necessary determination to pick ourselves up and go on until we at last persevere. Furthermore, as we strive, the journey will actually get easier for out of love, each time we tire, God will lift us and carry us part of the way until we are refreshed and re-energized!

Furthermore, as others join, our journey will become even easier as our brothers and sisters assist. They will offer a helping hand when we stumble in the same way we will offer a helping hand when they slip, trip or fall. And as the group grows and the process builds, the burden we initially felt will become instinctive and second nature such that we will no longer notice the weight of one of our brothers or sisters as we lift or carry them!

However, until our love can overwhelm our awareness of the difficulty of this journey of love, the trek is still worth it merely because of the amazing and miraculous fruits it will yield! In fact, the harvest it will yield will be unmatched in abundance. Why? Because per Fred Small, Senior Minister, First Parish, Cambridge, MA Unitarian-Universalist Church, "God's love is infinite and all-embracing. God's love does not discriminate. God's love does not reject..."[4]

It does not matter who or what you are (e.g. heterosexual, LGBT, black, white, hispanic, asian, young, old, male, female, rich or poor, or have pink or purple hair, etc. In addition, none of your genetic information makes a difference either) – "You are good. You are whole. You are of God, in God, with God, always..."[5]

Why? Because race, nationality, gender, age, sexual orientation, social status, disability (if applicable) as well as every other genetic trait make no difference to one's spirituality. And even if it did, which is not the case, God is always with you because His love never abandons or stops loving you, not even for a moment!

This is the true paradigm of God's love. It is not conditioned to or dependent upon human criteria. It is not subject to human judgement. It is not determined by our genetic code. It is simply and completely unconditional!

This is why God loves and saves everyone including victims of suicide among others. Even though they may have been spiritually, psychologically and/or physically battered, bruised and broken in this life, they are still loved by God!

Subsequently, to address this often painful and contentious issue – when a person dies of suicide, individuals, society and religious institutions must act with compassion since only God knows the pain that led to such an outcome. And because God alone knows the pain and He is love, the suicide victim too is saved through the Universal Savior.

Why? Because suicide is generally caused by mental illness, impulsiveness, unbearable pain, anguish, emotional and/or socio-economic burdens. In short, to put it in a more precise context, suicide in reality is a psychosomatic/socio-spiritual affliction. It is not a sin. It is not their fault. Therefore, the victim is not responsible since one does not commit suicide – one simply dies of it, in the same way one succumbs to any other disease or affliction.

Because of this, God will complete His loving plan of universal salvation in all, even if one's earthly mission is aborted abruptly by suicide. *"[H]e [W]ho began [the] good work in you will carry it on to completion..."* [Philippians 1:6]

In fact, with regard to Philippians 1:6, it is also evident that God out of love in the same context, even saves the unborn. It does not matter if a fetus is destroyed through miscarriage or abortion, the innocent unborn enjoy eternal life in heaven embraced by God's everlasting love in the same manner as the infants who were slaughtered in Bethlehem (c. 5 BCE) by order of Herod Antipas (20 BCE-39 CE) in his futile attempt to kill the Universal Savior whom he deemed as a threat to his rule over Galilee and Perea.

God's love is so great that His forgiveness of the woman who has an abortion does not nullify or contradict His love for the unborn and vice versa.

Rather, His love responds to that woman's intense pain all the while crying out for an end to abortion so that every conceived being may discover and know His love before life eternity and realize their potential through corporeal existence.

Imagine viewing an empty playground. The swings hang limp and motionless and a melancholy silence pervades where children's laughter ought to be joyfully bursting forth. Such is the toll of abortion, which is cold, unfeeling, and unloving.

While a woman has rights over her body (choice that includes protection from rape/incest and sexual abuse, protection from physical abuse that includes but is not limited to assault and genital mutilation, and the exercise of self-defense to protect her life and well-being), these rights in every possible case, should give the same respect to and afford the same recognition of the rights that the unborn baby has over his or her body.

There are, though extenuating circumstances such as when a woman's life is endangered by a pregnancy or in cases of rape/incest. However, with regard to the latter, it is my hope that in spite of the intense, indescribable hurt, the victim even through emotions of hate can find it in her heart to differentiate between the guilt of the perpetrator of that heinous act and the complete innocence of the fetus (who never asked to be created under these circumstances, whom God loves and in whom God also resides), and somehow summon the necessary strength and love to allow that baby to be born, even if he or she is given up for adoption afterwards.

I know it is not easy – those nine-months of love will be incredibly painful and difficult mentally and physically – in fact, they may be hell, but examples do exist of many women who have risen to the occasion and in the process been sanctified through this baptism by love – which is so much more painful than baptism by water and infinitesimally short of baptism by fire through martyrdom.

It is because of these woman who accept baptism by love in spite of the instinctive impulse, social pressure and so many other reasons to reject it that one may definitively and truly profess the courage of the saints with knowledge that many of their faces, names, and deeds are known only to God alone. Yet even if we do not know all these saints, God's love never forgets them since their courage enabled an innocent life to be born – in reality, the emergence of good from and the triumph of love over a horrible act of evil.

Prologue

The powerful testimony of Rebecca Kiessling (b. 1969 CE), who had been born to a mother who had twice considered an abortion after having been raped at knifepoint in 1968 CE, should give added reason for pause: "...I'd never considered that abortion applied to my life, but once... I realized that, not only does it apply to my life, but it has to do with my very existence... [i]t was as if I could hear the echoes of all... who, with the most sympathetic of tones, would say, 'Well, except in cases of rape...' or who would rather fervently exclaim in disgust: 'Especially in cases of rape!!!' All these people are out there who don't even know me, but are standing in judgment of my life, so quick to dismiss it just because of how I was conceived... [like] my life was... garbage – that I was disposable."[6]

I have mentioned suicide and abortion, because they are very relevant to God's love – He does not withdraw His love and salvation from the suicide victim, woman who has an abortion, and the unborn child – and because they are very personal to me.

One of my friends died of suicide in the 1980s CE following an argument with her parents over smoking a cigarette of all things. There is no way God her Father and Creator would turn His back and abandon her merely because of an impulsive, irreversible decision to jump from the 6th floor

xxv

window of her bedroom especially since His love is far greater than that of all biological and step-parents, past, present, and future put together!

I am also grateful for having been given out of God's *agape* love, the privilege to serve as His instrument, flawed as I am, to persuade two single, pregnant women out of having an abortion. In the first case, I asked a young teenaged woman to visualize the playground setting mentioned above. This was effective enough to bring about a sufficient change of heart such that she gave birth to a beautiful baby girl in early 1996 CE.

The second instance was more complex. This woman repeatedly insisted there was nothing I could say or do that would convince her to have the baby. So, I prayed that God take my life (even though at the time I was only in my 30s) in exchange that the baby be born and have a chance to live and experience life here on earth.

Afterwards, she did unexpectedly change her mind! Then when she was near term, I contracted chicken pox for the second time. Unlike the very mild barely noticeable case I had when I was young, – this occurrence was so severe (intense fever that would not break, delirium, chicken pox-related pneumonia, a failing liver, paralysis in my left arm) that as a last ditch, desperate effort, I was administered Acyclovir®, which at the time was often used to treat AIDS patients. Even then I was given little chance to survive.

However, a promise is a promise so in spite of the hidden weakness that filled my body when I heard one of the nurses say, "I don't think he'll make it through the night" – for *I did not really want to die so soon* – I did not regret my prayer of nine months earlier, which I had actually forgotten about until my illness.

During that darkest night of my illness, amidst prayers and my acceptance of God's loving will, I even wrote a poem that my brother of all things referred to as a "suicide note!" Part of it reads:

> *Let the will of God be done, let Him do unto me as He wills for I am His creation – given breath and life out of His unconditional generous love.*

> *Let the will of God be done, let Him do unto me as He wills, be I given trials or infirmity… I am joyful and grateful to receive my little cross!*

Out of love, God did extend my life since because of His love even when it appears only one of two alternatives are possible, God can make a third way! God's love is that powerful! It can make a way even when situations appear hopeless and impossible. In fact, God's love can make something out of nothing with creation being the greatest proof! Because of this, I want all to know just how great and loyal God's love truly is to each and every being of His creation!

Perhaps my life was extended to write this book so that all may truly know how great God's love is such that it unconditionally and eternally covers all of His creation past, present, and future!

In any event, my recovery began on the day this second beautiful baby girl was born in mid 1997 CE. I was discharged two days later with what I consider as a sign of God's indelible love – the chicken pox had formed a cross on my right wrist!

Finally, when I was leaving the hospital, it was really uplifting when an Indian nurse approached me and requested, "Please, pray for me!" – (a request that bridged the differences between my Christian faith and her Hindu faith). I guess I had kept my inner weakness sufficiently hidden!

With that said, the gates of heaven are open wide for all – the victim of suicide, the unborn baby, the woman who had an abortion, one who is LGBT. In fact they are open equally as wide for the murderous prisoner as the righteous saint since all persons upon passing have been purified by the blood of the Universal Savior and saved! No wonder God's ways are so much greater than ours!

At the same time while on the topic of love, I cannot omit the fact that God loves the disabled too especially since they glorify Him every second of their lives through their handicap. Mental or physical disability, it does not matter. Their lives are beatifically unified with that of the Universal Savior, the *"King of kings"* [Revelation 17:14] especially when he wore the crown of thorns. Through this beatific unification, they are sanctified through their figurative crown of thorns. Accordingly, through their crown, the disabled will inherit a great place in the heavenly kingdom.

In addition, the Universal Savior knows what it is like to be disabled. One can say, he experienced his own disability when he made the difficult trip to Calvary to fulfill God's salvific mission of love. While the will was there, his body failed him. As a result, he struggled, fell, and struggled again and fell again. After his third fall Jesus was assisted by Simon of Cyrene, which is no different than a physically or mentally challenged person being assisted by others!

The fact that Jesus allowed himself to experience physical disability prior to his crucifixion demonstrates God's great love for the disabled!

At the same time, to focus on the here and now, God's love for the disabled is also evident in the fact they live and breathe since life itself is created and sustained by God's love! God's love is also visible in their joy and happiness, in their struggles, as well as in their perseverance.

This is a wonderful thing considering that even those who are able-bodied will likely some day suffer a debilitating injury or illness and/or infirmity in old age. And when we do, God will not discard us. He will love us the same as we undergo our sanctification through our own crown of thorns – for the figurative thorns will hurt just the same as those that pierced the King's head.

In addition, one may also conclude that parents of the disabled who unceasingly love their child and care for him or her despite what at times appear to be insurmountable obstacles, are also sanctified. Like the mother who is a victim of rape and learns to love the innocent baby within her body, they too are sanctified through love because of their courage since it would be a lot easier to embrace loveless expedience and seek an abortion or abandon their child to an institution.

xxx

As the stepfather of a disabled child with cerebral palsy and psychological challenges, I know at times it can be very difficult and frustrating. However, at the same time, it can be very rewarding with many moments of joy. Regardless, the greatest incentive to persevere lies in the fact that life is precious, life is love, and love is God!

If this is not enough, consider the inspirational words of Bob Smith who requires total care, use of a motorized wheel chair and utilization of a Dynavox® speech generating device with a mouth-controlled stylus to communicate through a touch screen with programmable words – "Who am I? Not a vegetable... [A] person [with] feelings... You think I do not have a mind? You are wrong."[7] In addition, in spite of all, he is thankful for what God has given him and can say without hesitation, "God... loves us!"[8] This is why life is so precious and must never be discounted or discarded regardless of the circumstances.

With that said, it is also my hope that God is Love can bridge our differences, provide much needed hope to the alienated, serve as an instrument of God's love, and inspire and initiate positive change through tolerance, respect, strengthening of faith and a greater appreciation of God's love for each and every one of us. May God is Love serve as a much-needed light to eliminate today's darkness of hatred, intolerance, persecution, rejection, and abortion (with progress on the latter, save a life!) so that we may live in a just and peaceful world of tolerance, acceptance and love that promotes, protects and values each and every life so that the below scripture may be fulfilled:

"They will beat their swords into plowshares and their spears into pruning hooks. Nation will not take up sword against nation, nor will they train for war anymore." [Isaiah 2:4]

"The wolf will live with the lamb, the leopard will lie down with the goat, the calf and the lion and the yearling together... They will neither harm nor destroy..." [Isaiah 11:6 and 9]

Already, too many wars have been fought over nationalism and religion since the dawn of humanity. It is unacceptable that religious intolerance has been used to justify discrimination and genocidal violence costing more than 800 million lives. Nation and nation and religion and religion need not be in constant rivalry and war especially since God created all peoples and His love cries out for nothing less than harmonious peace!

God does not rejoice in violence, death and destruction for the attributes of His love are peace, life, and preservation – the foundation for universal salvation since anything less would fall short especially of the latter two.

Let *God is Love* facilitate the dawning of a new era in which, with our rich diversity, we not only coexist but interact with love, compassion, and righteousness such that the world is transformed into a holier, more sanctified place as we make our individual journeys to our inheritance – God's heavenly kingdom and eternal life – made possible only through His unconditional love that is epitomized by the Cross.

Perhaps one day all religions, despite their de facto autonomy may stand together in solidarity and pray together to magnify God's unconditional love for all.

Then we can have the world God so desires as we make our earthly journey and bide our time, all the while enriching the physical and spiritual lives of ourselves and others until we attain everlasting life in the heavenly kingdom.

Before I can conclude, I must also add that because of God's great love, plants and animals too will have a share in the afterlife despite flawed premises based on dualism (that postulates humans alone are sentient or self-aware and in possession of a soul) and species-based hubris, in which humans exalt themselves above every other living thing merely because we are in "God's image" based on Genesis 1:27. True, we are in God's image but that does not make us any better or more deserving of salvation for no one and nothing is deserving of salvation. We only attain it because of God's salvific love. Furthermore, the fact we are in "God's image" only means we have a special calling to spread His love above and beyond that of every other living being!

Nevertheless, as science advances, it is becoming increasingly apparent that an expanding list of living creatures (e.g. dolphins, chimpanzees, elephants, whales, and even birds, to name just a few) possess sentience.

In addition, with regard to possession of a soul, Greek philosopher Aristotle (384-322 BCE) wrote, "soul is… life upon a body… enabling the living being to engage in its various functions."[9] Had there been no soul in an animal or plant, its body would be lifeless.

This is consistent with both Western (e.g. Judaism, Christianity, and Islam) and Eastern (e.g. Buddhism, Hinduism, and Jainism to name a few) religions. Eastern religions state that every living thing – plants, animals and humans – possess an "*atman*" or "divine soul."[10] At the same time, from a

Western view, the phrase "animating principle" is derived from the Latin term "*anima,*" which is referred to as "*soul*" in a Christian context. At the same time, the Hebrew term "*nephesh chayah*" is used to describe animals and people alike in Old Testament Jewish writings. Only English versions of the Bible make delineation using the phrase "living creature" for animals and "living soul" for humans.[11]

Scripture provides further proof that plants and animals will attain the heavenly kingdom:

"*...None of these* (referring to plants and animals alike) *will be missing...*" [Isaiah 34:16]

"*The armies of heaven were... riding on white horses*" [Revelation 19:14]

As can be attained from the above scriptural passages and Isaiah 11:6 and 9 mentioned above, all creatures will attain eternal salvation. Otherwise how could the armies of heaven ride horses, paradise consist of plants and animals, and every living creature get along in the "new" earth?

Also from a purely aesthetic sense, heaven would be a barren place lacking the unspeakable beauty that a broad spectrum of religions describe, if it did not include plants and animals!

William Sutherland

If further proof is needed, Buddhism describes heaven as more breathtaking than a *"Holy Land exquisitely adorned with gold and silver and precious gems [that consists of] pure waters with golden sands, surrounded by pleasant walks covered with lotus flowers [in which] [j]oyous music is heard... flowers rain down three times a day [and the] birds sing... harmonious notes* [in praise of God].*"*[12]

Likewise from a Western and indigenous perspective – heaven consists of a garden based on Christianity: Revelation 22 that describes heaven as a city with a garden that includes a river and a *"tree of life"* with *"twelve crops of fruit,"* Islam: The Cave 18:31 that describes heaven as a place with *"gardens of perpetuity"* and Judaism: Kabbalah that states the third out of seven heavens is *"the home of the 'Garden of Eden'"* that harbored animal life in Genesis and the *"tree of life."*[13] In addition, heaven is filled with animal spirits based on Native American, animist and other indigenous writings.

Best of all, every person will be reunited with family, friends, and pets in the afterlife since God's love would have it no other way especially since He knows our love for family, friends, and pets. God's love would not and could not violate our love through deprivation and separation, nor exclude

xxxvi

classes of living things from salvation since then it would revert to cruelty, which is not possible!

Last but not least, if plants and animals did not attain a share of eternal life, the Universal Savior's victory over death would have been limited and incomplete, which we know not to be the case based on 1 Corinthians 15:53-54 – *"Death has been swallowed up in victory."*

Finally, may *God is Love* illuminate God's love so that all may discover there is every reason for hope and none for despair, for out of love God sent forth the Universal Savior of Himself to unleash universal salvation to save each and every conceived soul. Sin and death have been defeated! The victory is complete! All creation has been saved! All are loved and will attain eternal life in God's kingdom of everlasting love!

May God in His everlasting, unconditional *agape* love bless and keep you and your friends and family and all creation always. May God's love give you the courage to love as He does – especially those who are scorned and rejected by society or different from you. And most importantly, may you always know you are always loved and let this book remind you if you should forget,

William

[1] Patrick Ahern. Maurice and Thérèse: The Story of Love. Image Publishing, Inc., Memphis, TN. 2001.

[2] Louis Henkin. Religion, Religions, and Human Rights. The Journal of Religious Ethics. Vol. 26, No. 2. Fall 1998. 231.

[3] Bahá'u'lláh. The Hidden Words. Wilmette: Baha' Publishing Trust, 1985, Arabic #68. 20.

[4] Standing on the Side of Love. Facebook. 25 August 2013. https://www.facebook.com/SideofLove/posts/190362511039210

[5] Standing on the Side of Love. Facebook. 25 August 2013. https://www.facebook.com/SideofLove/posts/190362511039210

[6] Rebecca Kiessling. Conceived in Rape. Targeted for Abortion. 2 September 2013. http://www.rebeccakiessling.com/Othersconceivedinrape.html

[7] Bob Smith. Reflections Of My Life. 2013. 15. To order copies, contact Ralph Szur at 914-949-9300, ext. 3002.

[8] Bob Smith. Reflections Of My Life. 2013. 3, 13. To order copies, contact Ralph Szur at 914-949-9300, ext. 3002.

[9] Ronald Polansky. Aristotle's De Anima. Cambridge University Press. New York. September 2007.

[10] Soul. Wikipedia.org. 10 July 2011. http://en.wikipedia.org/wiki/Soul

[11] Animals in The Afterlife. Lites of Heaven. 2007-2011.
http://www.litesofheaven.com/animalsintheafterlife.html

[12] Buddhist Prophesies Fulfilled. 28 March 2011.
http://www.bci.org/prophecy-fulfilled/Buddha.htm

[13] Heaven. Wikipedia.org. 9 July 2011.
http://en.wikipedia.org/wiki/Heaven#Rabbinical_Judaism

Additional Sources:

Black Gopnik. Clash of the Titans. Newsweek. 9 April 2012.
55.

Donald L. Mosher, Ph. D. Commentary: Threat to Sexual
Freedom: Moralistic Intolerance Instills a Spiral of Silence. The
Journal of Sex Research. Vol. 26, No. 4. November 1989.

Helen C. Evans and William D. Wixom. The Glory of
Byzantium. The Metropolitan Museum of Art. 1997. 365.

Muhammad ibn Sulayman at-Tameemi. Mukhtasar Seeratur
Rasool.

seehowtheyrun. Huffington Post. 22 July 2006.
http://www.huffingtonpost.com/social/seehowtheyrun/general-
david-petraeus-co_n_706718_59632884.html

God is Love

"God is love." The concept and reality of God's very essence is so important that it is mentioned not once, but twice in the Bible. Both 1 John 4:8 and 1 John 4:16 declare *"God is love"* refuting descriptions rendered by the ancients that viewed Him as vengeful, jealous, demanding, and eager to punish.

God is the Eternal Light – *"I am the way, the truth, and the light"* [John 14:6], *"The Lord is my Light and my Salvation..."* [Psalm 27:1], The Light 24:35 *"[God] is the Light of the heavens and the earth..."* [Islam], and *"God is the Unbounded Light."*[1] [Buddhism]

In fact, love is the "manifestation of the Truth" [Bahai'ism][2] and the sole reason for our existence. Per Evangelical pastor Rick Warren (1954- CE), God, Who is love "...didn't need us. But [H]e wanted us."[3]

"I knew My love for thee... therefore I created thee..." [Bahai'ism][4]

1

"I AM therefore you are. I AM LOVE – DIVINE LOVE. I [l]ove you with an infinite and therefore perfect [l]ove... You are [l]oved into being."[5]

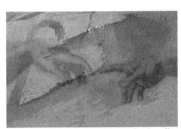

"You are [l]oved into being"

"And the LORD God... breathed into his nostrils the breath of life..." [Genesis 2:7] And what did God breathe in? Love because *"[l]ove is the breath of the Holy Spirit..."*[6] [Bahai'ism: Abdu'l-Bahá (1844-1921 CE), Tablets of Abdu'l-Bahá v. 3 1]

"God's love has been poured into our hearts through the Holy Spirit, who has been given to us." [Romans 5:5]

In reality, everything of God is love because "He is love itself"[7] such that 100% of His being is composed of love! Every Divine particle is love!

Thus, "[t]he Lord created... because... Love seeks to make others outside of self happy."[8]

2

God through His love is compassionate, merciful, and forgiving. His "love permeates all religions."[9] He is not the "God" depicted by ancient writers who attached flawed human characteristics to His Being. The words of St. Augustine (354-430 CE) can attest to this – "God… our knowledge of [Y]ou is imperfect. In our ignorance we have… wrongly thought that [Y]ou take pleasure in punishing us for our sins; and we have foolishly conceived [Y]ou to be a tyrant over human life."[10]

Therefore, when scriptural messages, regardless of religion are divisive, ethnocentric, and promote intolerance and discrimination they do not reflect God's true nature of love. Instead, they are merely the product of misinterpretation and subjective perception expressed by imperfect messengers due to human fallibility.

In reality, God unleashed His creative powers as an expression of His Infinite love – "*God created the world because love needs another to love.*"[11] [Judaism: Kabbalah] This was immediately evident when God had created the first being based on *A Limb Just Moved* by Brahmin princess and Hindu mystic Mirabai (1498-1547 CE) – "And You practiced Your love in the hearts of animals before You created man…"[12]

3

William Sutherland

Furthermore, "Love is the gravity that pulls the universe together."[13] Consequently, with creation in place to love, God gives us an *easy yoke and light burden"* [Matthew 11:30] after having offered Himself as the Universal Savior, an act that extends beyond the limits of any single religion or branch of faith and can be described as divine "[l]ove... of heaven to earth come down," to use the words of Anglican clergyman Charles Wesley (1707-1788 CE).[14] The incarnation was more than the "word made flesh" as described in John 1:14 – it was divine love come to earth in corporeal flesh!

Love was the flesh that suffered through the scourging and crucifixion. Love was the body that died on the cross. Love was the spirit that resurrected.

Why? Because, *"[t]here is no greater love than to lay down one's life for one's friends"* [John 15:13] and God could not create a single living organism without the prospect of salvation. Because of this, even though God could have granted salvation through any other means, He chose crucifixion on a cross since it consisted of extreme humiliation and suffering prior to death. He wanted to punctuate His love with an exclamation mark! For Him, there was no other way!

4

"Love suffers..." [1 Corinthians 13:4]

Love suffers because it is so profound such that real pain is inflicted when it is not reciprocated, is betrayed or its beloved suffers. Yet, in spite of God's eternal *agape* love, we constantly betray Him through sin or acts of injustice/evil as well as through apathy and indifference (since the latter two constitute a failure to love) because of our weak human nature. Add the number of people who suffer through disaster, disease, or injustice as well as those who reject God through alienation and/or atheism and it gets even worse.

Thus per Søren Kierkegaard (1813-1855 CE), a Danish philosopher and theologian, "God is love... You cannot even remotely imagine how He suffers. For He knows how difficult and painful it is for you. But He can change nothing of it, since otherwise He Himself would have to become something different, something other than love."[15]

Because of this, Plato's (427-347 BCE) words in the *Phaedrus* resonate – "[L]ove is... the great divine madness."[16] From an earthly perspective – "The cross is madness. Loving your enemies is madness."[17] Turning the other cheek is madness. But such is the nature of God's love – "[I]t goes beyond logic. If it were perfectly sensible it would be given only to those who deserved it. But... it flows out freely..."[18] Consequently, since *"God is love"* [1 John 4:8 and 16] and *"Love is the light of the Kingdom"* [Bahai'ism], Italian Jewish philosopher Yochanan Allemano (1435-1504 CE), wrote, "dazzling bright, like the light of the sun, is the sweetness of divine madness."[19]

So when the question is asked – "If God is so powerful, why couldn't He have given salvation some other way?" – Know, the answer is not a mystery except to one who does not or cannot fully grasp even a tiny portion of the depth and magnitude of God's very Being. It is simple. He could have but He did not because it was not about His omnipotent power, might or strength. It was about love! He is love and it was out of love He chose to give of Himself the Universal Savior and thus die on a cross. Otherwise His love would not have been the greatest – a contradiction of the infallible truth, the infinite opposite of His nature, and a denial of His very Self! There is no greater love and that is God Who never stops loving, not even for a moment!

Perhaps this was the inspiration for William Shakespeare (1564-1616 CE) when he wrote in *Romeo and Juliet* – "My bounty is as boundless as the sea. My love as deep; the more I give to thee, [t]he more I have, for both are infinite."[20]

Besides, despite human connotations that grandeur is associated with power, strength, and might, to the Divine, "Love is where the glory falls" [Sufism: Khāja Shamsu Dīn Muhammad Hāfez-e Shīrāzī (1325-1389 CE)] because, "'...[M]y thoughts are not your thoughts, neither are your ways [M]y ways,' says the LORD. 'For as the heavens are higher than the earth, so are [M]y ways higher than your ways, and [M]y thoughts than your thoughts'." [Isaiah 55:8-9]

Per Sufi poet Jalāl ad-Dīn Muhammad Rūmī (1207-1273 CE), "The lover is a king above all kings."

Consequently, it is not surprising that God Who is the greatest Lover as demonstrated through the Universal Savior is not a King above all kings but *the* King of kings – "*On his robe and on his thigh he has this name written: King of Kings...*" [Revelation 19:16]

In fact God's love is so great that *"[e]ven the prayers of an ant reach heaven."*[21] [Shintoism] No prayer, no matter how insignificant it may appear, is unimportant to God!

William Sutherland

Per Pope (St.) John Paul II (1920-2005 CE), God's love "is so great that it goes beyond the limits of human language, beyond the grasp of artistic expression, beyond human understanding."[22]

Likewise, God's love is *agape* since anything short would limit it. Thus by its very definition, God's love "is pure... [and] unlimited in its possibilities. [It] is altruistic... [and] given for its own sake, without expecting anything in return." It is unconditional and extended to "every [living] being" without exception.[23] It is, in the words of Brazilian novelist Paulo Coelho (1947- CE), *The* Pilgrimage – "the love that consumes... the highest and purest form of love... a selfless love..." that per American writer C.S. Lewis (1898-1963 CE), *The Four Loves*, is "committed to the well-being of... other[s]."[24] In fact God's love is so ineffably great, He is known as "al-Wadud" or "He who loves"[25] in Islam and "Pure Love"[26] in Hinduism, Jainism, Buddhism, and Sikhism.

Per Sufi St. Rābi'ah al-Basrī (717–801 CE) in *The Perfect Stillness*, "Love is the... most profound act, and the word [is] almost as complete as His name."[27] Accordingly, it can be said as written by Swedish scientist, philosopher, theologian and founder of The New Church, Emanuel Swedenborg

(1688-1772 CE) in *Divine Love 2. [3.] II* (1762-1763 CE) – "The Lord alone is love itself."

Consistent with Swedenborg's premise, Anglican theologian Oliver C. Quick (1885-1944 CE) wrote, "If we could imagine the love of one who loves men purely for their own sake, and not because of any need or desire of his own, purely desires their good, and yet loves them wholly, not for what at this moment they are, but for what he knows he can make of them because he made them, then we should have in our minds some true image of the love of the Father and Creator of mankind."[28]

Unlike human love, God's love endures all things and "never fail[s] or lose[s] its glory."[29] Furthermore it embraces all of His creation – The Believer 40:7 *"You embrace all things within Your love..."* [Islam]

"Pen and ink shall pass away, along with what has been written... [T]he love of God shall never perish." [Sikhism – Sri Guru Granth Sahib]

"O give thanks to the Lord... for [H]is steadfast love endures forever." [Psalm 136:1]

Per Baptist minister Job Hupton (1762-1829 CE), "What [God] is, [H]e ever was, and ever will be (which is love) ... there can be no variation."[30]

9

God's eternal nature of love never changes. There is no beginning or end to God's love, which may be described as an eternal well of giving. Why? Because as God is moved by our needs, petitions and emotions (especially pain and suffering), He pours out even more love!

Therefore, "[w]hat are termed the grace, the mercy, the pity, and the kindness of the Lord... [are merely] many modifications of the manifestation of [H]is love."[31] In fact, every act of God and everything Divine is love!

And as mentioned above, since God is moved by His creation, His love is dynamic. It is responsive to and is "influenced by those who are loved,"[32] which means each and every being of creation.

"He was moved with compassion..." [Matthew 9:36] is just one such example of God being responsive to and influenced by His creation. However, the examples are so numerous they range from infinity (∞) minus 1 to ∞. The former relates to all creation within their natural state that are constrained within a finite number of universes subject to space and time and the latter to life eternal that is not confined by time nor space. Accordingly, per Baptist minister and theologian Augustus Strong (1836-1921 CE) – "God is eternally moved."[33] Out of

love, He is moved by our acts, words, needs, insecurities, emotions, and aspirations, the latter, which includes (whether or not we consciously think about it) eternal salvation – the ultimate end to every being's natural existence, which can be and is only possible simply because "God is love." [1 John 4:8 and 16]

At the same time, God's love survives beyond time and space and cannot be limited or reduced by changing society, human words, actions or moral standards nor, in the words of British author, Arthur C. Clarke (1917-2008 CE), "collision with the truth"[34] for it is the undeniable, infallible truth. This is why Jesus preached, "[L]ove your enemies" [Matthew 5:44] during his Sermon on the Mount. Even hatred and iniquity directed at the Universal Savior could not limit, reduce or erase the love of God. Divine love burned in Christ's heart and encapsulated every cell in his body, which as the manifestation of God Himself was love itself! Thus Jesus even loved each and every person involved in his crucifixion. He loved Judas Iscariot (c. 1 BCE-33 CE)! He loved Pontius Pilate, prefect of Judea from 26-36 CE! He loved Herod Antipas (20 BCE-39 CE), ruler of Galilee and Perea! He loved Joseph Caiaphas, high priest from 18-37 CE! He loved the Sanhedrin that condemned him, the Roman soldiers that mocked and scourged him,

William Sutherland

drove nails into his body and opened his side with a
lance as well as the crowd that jeered him, spit at
him and cried out, *"Crucify him!"* [Mark 15:13]
Anything less would have undermined the infallible
truth of God's love!

Likewise, God's *agape* love is the cornerstone of
John 3:16-17 – *"For God so loved the world, that
[H]e gave [H]is only begotten Son... not... to
condemn the world, but to save the world through
him."*

It is also because of this love that God gave us
knowledge such that when used in conformance
with His will, it advances technology to enhance
medical treatment (e.g. to treat disease as well as
to enable the barren to have children), reduces
hunger (e.g. through creation of drought-and-pest
resistant plants), advances tolerance, ethical,
philosophical, and theological understandings and
improves standards of living.

*Al-Sajdah 32:7 He is the One [W]ho... Al-Sajdah 32:9 gave
you the hearing, the eyesight, and the brains...*
[Islam]

Therefore, religion and science need not be
antagonistic since science not only seeks to explain
how God does things but it actually affirms His very

existence and confirms He is the author of all things.

Prior to the "Big Bang," which can be described as an unprecedented and unmatched explosion, there was nothing – an infinite, dark, empty, inert void. Yet the laws of science state something cannot be created from nothing. Add the facts that our universe is approximately 13.7 billion years old and the "Big Bang" created matter, anti-matter and energy that led to the subsequent creation of elements, organic compounds, water and ultimately life itself from the infinite, dark, empty, inert void and there can only be one plausible scientific explanation – God is the singular constant that has always existed separate from all the universes, Who out of love initiated the "Big Bang" to begin creation.

At the same time, when God created humans, the first pair were undoubtedly adults in whom He imparted sufficient knowledge so they could survive. Had it been any different, the results would have been abysmal and humans would have died out in a matter of days, if that long. Just imagine a newborn baby, who is most vulnerable and helpless and you can picture the outcome. Thus the creation of the first man and woman as adults is further proof that God's hand and not some random phenomena of nature is the origin of not only human life, but all life and every particle of matter, anti-matter, and energy.

When considering how God created life, one may use computers as an analogy especially since before they are programmed, they are useless boxes of circuitry.

Since life is vastly more complex than the most advanced computer – its programming language is likewise considerably more complex. While computer language is based on binary code of 0s and 1s, the language of life (DNA) utilizes four base acids – A (adenine), C (cytosine), G (guanine), and T (thymine). Furthermore, while binary code is one-dimensional, life's code is three-dimensional utilizing a double helix whose base pairs determine our every characteristic, trait and most importantly enable us to possess and exercise free will. Thus, DNA in essence, is God's software for life.

Consistent with binary code that is consciously written with a given purpose, God's code too has been carefully, consciously, cognitively, and lovingly created for each living organism. Neither code – binary nor DNA, created itself by chance or by accident, which is further proof that God's hand is responsible for the creation of each and every form of life.

Al-Sajdah 32:9 *"[God] shaped him and blew into him from His spirit."* [Islam]

A computer analogy may also be used here. When God "blew" love into His creation, He literally powered it on – initiating the metabolic activities of our lives – in the same way we power up a computer by pushing the "on" button.

Furthermore, per St. Thomas Aquinas (1225-1274 CE), "[s]ince human beings are said to be in the image of God in virtue of their having nature that includes an intellect, such a nature is most in the image of God in virtue of being most able to imitate God... [He] created both us and the world, and arranged for the former to know the latter" and since it is through science that we "acquire knowledge of ourselves and the world,"[35] scientific research and technological advancements are clearly a part of God's loving plan Why? Because "[l]ove and understanding are indissolubly linked."[36]

God's *agape* love is also the reason why we are His son's and daughter's and ultimately heirs to an inheritance of eternal life in His heavenly kingdom that is free of evil, the stain of sin, pain, suffering, infirmity, and every other negative thing.

15

William Sutherland

Accordingly, as the first step, God pronounced all creation good[37] – *"God saw all that [H]e had made, and it was very good."* [Genesis 1:31] and *"[His] works are righteous."* [Hinduism: Rig Veda Hymn LXXXI. Visvakarman]

"...[Y]ou are no longer a slave, but a [child]; and since you are a [child], God has made you also an heir." [Galatians 4:7]

"God... has given me His Hand... [He] has made me His Own... He has blessed me with eternal life." [Sikhism – Sri Guru Granth Sahib]

Because of this, we are all brothers and sisters and children of the same God of love. We are all heirs to the Kingdom.

In addition, we are all in the image of God and share the same DNA such that there is but one race – the human race.

"All [are] sisters and brothers from a common [D]ivine [S]ource reaching out to a common [D]ivine destiny... All beings emanate from One and return to One." [38] [Cao Daism]

Therefore, in the words of the *Saman Suttam* (a text created by a committee of representatives from

16

all the major sects of Jainism in 1974 CE[39]) and St. Clement of Alexandria (c. 150-215 CE), respectively – *"Killing a living being is killing one's own self; showing compassion to a living being is showing compassion to oneself…"* [Verse 151 – Jainism] and "When you see your brother [or sister], you see God."[40]

Likewise, each person is anointed by the Holy Spirit such that "religions are not entities unto themselves; they are part of the experience of people living them" and thus "living, [breathing] entities."[41] In short, God resides in each and every person – *"Do you not know that your bodies are temples of the Holy Spirit, who is in you, whom you have received from God?"* [1 Corinthians 6:19]

"Great Spirit is the life that is in all things."[42] [Rolling Thunder (1916-1997 CE)]

"God resides in each of us."[43] [Cheondoism]

"Within this earthen vessel… is the Creator…"[44] [Sufism: Kabir (1440-1518 CE)]

"Do not search in distant skies for God. In [a person's] own heart is He found."[45] [Shintoism]

17

"The heart is the sanctuary of God..."[46] [Islam: Imam Ja'far al-Sadiq (702-765 CE)]

"My Beloved dwells in my heart."[47] [Hinduism: Mirabai]

"[God] dwells deep within the nucleus of all beings." [Sikhism: Sri Guru Granth Sahib]

And since *"God is love"* [1 John 4:8 and 16], in the words of British Eastern Orthodox bishop Kallistos Ware (1934- CE), "In its deepest sense, love is the life, the energy, of the Creator in us."

Consistent with these facts, God is both present in and the center of all religions since His absence would constitute a degradation of His *agape* love. In fact as God's presence is most pronounced in the diversity of peoples, His love is greatest in the diversity of religions when viewed as a whole – "Religion is love and love is religion."[48] [Islam: Imam al-Baqir (676-733 CE)] Thus, He is an "inclusivist" God such that all, including those who practice non-Christian religions (e.g. other Abrahamic – Judaism and Islam, as well as Eastern non-Abrahamic faiths) are saved through Christ, the Universal Savior since as was mentioned earlier, God wills to save all since after all, He is love.

18

"Says the Lord: `[A]ll... enjoy my ministry of mercy.'" [49] [Shintoism]

"Of every kind of sin Thou art atonement... Of all sins Thou art atonement." [Hindusim: Yajur Veda 8.13]

"I am [H]e [W]ho blots out your transgressions... and remembers your sins no more." [Isaiah 43:25]

"However innumerable beings are, I vow to save them." [50] [Buddhism]

An "exclusivist" approach that solely renders Christians "saved" and non-Christians "unsaved" not only contradicts God's *agape* love but also diminishes the power of the cross and Christ's resurrection. Jesus made it clear, *"...[W]ith God all things are possible."* [Matthew 19:26] He did not say "most things" or "some things" are possible with God because God's power and love cannot be limited!

Thus forget about false distinctions between "saved" and "unsaved." All are saved by the Universal Savior – the epic manifestation of God's love such that there is no such thing as an "unsaved" person.

19

Accordingly, Jewish philosopher Chasdai Crescas (1340-1410 CE) wrote, "Salvation is attained... solely by the love of God."[51]

Consequently, Thomas Talbott, Professor Emeritus of Philosophy at Willamette University, Salem, OR wrote:

...[T]he Western theological tradition seemed to leave me with a choice between an unjust and unloving God, on the one hand, and a defeated God, on the other. But of course this hardly exhausts the logical possibilities; there remains the additional possibility that it is God's very nature to love, as 1 John 4:8 and 16 appears to declare, and that [H]e is also wise and resourceful enough to accomplish all of [H]is loving purposes in the end. Why... after all, should an assumption concerning everlasting punishment be the only unquestioned assumption in a context where some are limiting the extent of God's love and others are limiting the scope of [H]is ultimate victory?

...I now view universal reconciliation... as essential to a proper understanding of salvation...[52]

In fact universal reconciliation is the only possibility when the true nature and extent of God's love is considered.

"God is perfectly and universally loving and merciful."[53] His love is without blemish such that nothing can approach it. Precisely for this reason, it is extended to all and will ultimately save all.

Thus it is a mistake to believe that one may only attain salvation through acceptance of a single religion or specific theological dogma. In the words of John Hick, theologian and philosopher (1922-2012 CE), the world's different religions "have conceived of and experienced the one ultimate divine Reality... constitut[ing] a valid context of salvation."[54] Therefore, as all religions are branches of the same vine with "facets of the same, one truth,"[55] God offers each of us a unique, multi-dimensional personal relationship such that His message, though consistent with His loving nature and scripture (regardless of religion), will be different. His message is individualized towards our personal needs to enhance our spiritual growth and facilitate our personal journey of discovery so that our path to salvation may be broadened.

For this reason, there is no need to convert from one religion to another or to chase after other religions since all lead to love and ultimately draw one closer to God. Your religion, theological beliefs and faith are sufficient in and of themselves to have a loving, salvific relationship with God.

In short, "[t]here are many paths to the one God, and no matter what name people choose to call Him, we all worship the same God of Love."[56]

"Howsoever [people] approach Me, even so, do I welcome them, for the path [they] take from every side is Mine..." [57] [Hinduism]

"Your door is open to all..."[58] [Sufism: St. Rābi'ah al-Basrī]

Therefore God's love is visible in comparative theology, the simplicity of His laws, and the gift of Himself as the Universal Savior.

Comparative Theology:

God's *"agape"* love is the unifying factor of the world's religions such that when all religions are considered, they provide a broader picture of His love than a single religion ever could ("The big picture" vs. a tiny microcosm). This is the rationale of 2nd Century CE Rabbi Shimon Ben Zoma when he said, "Who is wise? He who learns from all..."

22

However, in order to do so, one must "not be [so] conscious of his own [religion] as to refuse to lower himself to seek knowledge from [another]." [Judaism: Pirkei Avot]

Accordingly, St. Thomas Aquinas even warned against the close-minded individual that seeks to limit God's salvific love to a specific or single faith, "Beware of the person of one book."[59] Why? First, according to St. Thomas Aquinas, "[e]very truth without exception – no matter who makes it – is from God."[60]

Second, one must not surrender objectivity to personal biases such that they insist their religion and beliefs comprise the sole and only viable path to God's love and salvation.

Per Evangelical writer Jerry Bridges (1947- CE), "Our doubts do not destroy God's love, nor does our faith create it."[61] It exists with or without faith for it always was and always will be! This is precisely the reason why God loves atheists too even if they do not recognize Him or His love!

"[T]he Supreme Being is the source of the world's... religions..."[62] [Cao Daism] such that *"[a]ll the... religions of the world, and their sacred texts, have worth."*[63] [Unitarian-Universalist]

23

As a result, "[a]ll religions [are] basically one, different variations on an identical theme, manifold manifestations of one and the same [E]ssence"[64] – God Who is love.

God's love is so great it is omnipresent. It is everywhere! It is found in every faith, it is found in every deed of compassion, every act of virtue, in every species (even if through their mere being) and in every feeling, expression and shared moment of love. It is not confined by space, distance or time.

"Where love is, there God is also." [Mohatma Gandhi (1869-1948 CE)][65]

Per John Templeton, *Agape Love* (1999 CE), "[t]he rich variety of world religions creates a tapestry of amazing beauty" that exhibits "God's *agape* love" towards "all of creation."

God views all life as equally precious and sacred and worthy of preservation since it involved His creative action and consists of a "part of the divine soul."[66] Accordingly, out of love, God maintains a special relationship with each of His creation.

"...God created man in His own image... male and female He created them." [Genesis 1:27] *"You*

24

created my inmost being; [Y]ou knit me together in my mother's womb." [Psalm 139:13] *"Do we not all have one Father?"* [Malachi 2:10]

"[God] created... all from the same dust..." [Bahai'ism]

"All souls are alike... None is superior or inferior."[67] [Jainism: Mahavira Vardhamana (599-527 BCE)]

Al-Sajdah 32:7 *"...He created, and started the creation of the human from clay.* Al-Sajdah 32:9 *He shaped him and blew into him from His spirit. And He gave you...* The Romans 30:22 *the diversity of your tongues and colors."* [Islam]

All are created equally:

The Book of Imran 3:195 *"I will not lose sight of the labor of any of you who labors in My way, be it man or woman; each of you is equal to the other."* [Islam]

"...[T]he seeds of the kingdom are planted in both women and men... [I]n the kingdom there is no difference..." [The "Luminous" Religion (practiced in China from c. 635-1399 CE before being stamped out by oppression and persecution in mid-to-late 14th century CE)]

"We... are clay blended by the Master Potter, come from the kiln of Creation in many hues... What should it matter that one bowl is dark and the other pale, if each is of good design and serves its purpose well." [North American Indian: Polingaysi Qoyawayma, Hopi]

Based on the above scriptures and sayings that show God deliberately created us with diversity, loves and values us equally, and includes each and every one of us in His plan of universal salvation, it can be said that the continuum of Divine love is composed of diversity, equality and inclusion.

"Each person, because of her/his humanity inherently has dignity and worth."[68] [Unitarian-Universalism]

"[T]he laws of God forbid [people] [t]o destroy [their] own kind... [and] [t]o... enslave [others]... ...[A]ll [people] of whatever race, color or creed were created with equal rights..." [Scientology]

The Acaranga Sutra goes even further and states, *"Nothing which breathes, which exists, which lives, or which has essence or potential of life, should be destroyed or ruled over, or subjugated, or harmed, or denied of its essence or potential."* [Jainism]

The "Sanctity of Life"

Why? Because all creation has priceless worth or "sanctity of life." This infinite worth is attributable solely to the fact that *"God is love"* [1 John 4:8 and 16], the basis of St. Teresa of Ávila's (1515-1582 CE) quote – "It is love alone that gives worth to all things."[69]

Consistent with this, *"God's compassion extends to all… His works."* [Judaism: Talmud Midrach Sifre to Bamidbar 27] and *"…is equal for [all]."* [North American Indian]

"[God] is the source of loving-kindness…"[70] [African Indigenous Religions]

"[God is the] Lord of love… He Who is permanently benign." [Ancient Egyptian theology][71]

27

William Sutherland

The ^{Elevated Places 7:156} "My love embraces all things."
[Islam]

Accordingly, "Heaven covers all without partiality; earth sustains and embraces without partiality; the sun and the moon shine upon all without partiality." [Confucianism]

"The [S]upreme [G]ood (God) nourishes all things without trying to."[72] [Taoism]

Sufi ascetic Bayazid Bastami (804-874 CE) captured the essence of God's love when he wrote: "At the beginning I was mistaken... I concerned myself to remember God, to know Him, to love Him and to seek Him. When I had come to the end I saw that He had remembered me before I remembered Him, that His knowledge of me had preceded my knowledge of Him, that His love towards me had existed before my love to Him and He had sought me before I sought Him."[73]

"I sought the Lord, and afterward I knew... It was not I that found... For Thou wert long beforehand with my soul, [a]lways Thou lovest me."[74] [Lutheran Hymn]

28

Simplicity of God's Laws:

God's love is exemplified by the simplicity of His laws (e.g. The Ten Commandments, Two Great Commandments, and Golden Rule, the latter which is found in every religion and ethical tradition including the secular, leading to the Universal Principle – *"[T]reat others as we wish others to treat us"* – that was adopted by 143 respected religious leaders from the Baha'i Faith, Brahmanism, Brahma Kumaris, Buddhism, Christianity, Hinduism, Indigenous, Interfaith, Islam, Jainism, Judaism, Native American, Neo-Pagan, Sikhism, Taoism, Theosophist, Unitarian Universalist and Zoroastrian in the "Declaration Toward a Global Ethic" in 1993 CE), which are kept to the optimal minimum.

Two Great Commandments: (Christianity – Matthew 22:37 and 39; Judaism – Deuteronomy 6:5 and Leviticus 19:18)   1. "Love the Lord your God with all your heart and with all your soul and with all your mind."   2. "Love your neighbor as yourself."

Ten Commandments: (Christianity, Islam, Judaism, the "Luminous" Religion, 6, 8-9 applicable to Buddhism and Jainism)

1. "I am the LORD your God... You shall have no other gods before Me."
2. "Do not make idols of any kind."
3. "Do not take the name of the LORD your God in vain."
4. "Remember the Sabbath day... keep it holy."
5. "Honor your father and your mother."
6. "You shall not kill" – *Ahimsa.*
7. "You shall not commit adultery."
8. "You shall not steal" – *Asteya.*
9. "You shall not bear false witness" – *Satya.*
10. "You shall not covet your neighbor's house... your neighbor's wife... [your] neighbor's children]... nor anything that is your neighbor's."

God's Laws

In addition, as *"God is love"* [1 John 4:8 and 16], all of His commandments can be fulfilled through love.

"[L]ove is the fulfilling of the law." [Romans 13:10]

"...[A]ll the law is fulfilled in one word... love..." [Galatians 5:14]

God through His love desires that all be saved. Therefore He did not want to create rules that were hopelessly impossible to follow. *"...My yoke is easy and My burden is light."* [Matthew 11:30] Even then, as we often fall short, *"[w]e are saved by the grace of God, not by works."* [Ephesians 2:8-9] Had salvation been solely contingent upon works, God would be quite lonely for heaven would be quite empty since it would be impossible for anyone to be saved!

Why? Because no one is perfect and no one is capable of permanent abstinence from sin after repenting. This includes all the saints who continually strived to perfect themselves during their earthly existence since it is the predisposition of our flawed and weak human nature to fall back into sin despite our sincerest and best efforts to avoid it.

31

Accordingly, when following God's commandments, all one needs to do is love, which entails forgiving, and abstinence from judging as exemplified by the mercy Jesus directed towards the adulterous woman. When Jesus was asked if she should be stoned, he replied, *"Whoever among you is without sin, let him cast the first stone"* [John 8:7] before finishing, *"Neither do I condemn you."* [John 8:11]

We are called to love based on the question of Sri Guru Granth Sahib (Var. Sarang, p. 1237) – *"Whom should I despise, since the one Lord made us all?"* [Sikhism]

Thus we must in the words of Jesus, *"Look for the best in others and correct what is worst in yourself... Think not of the faults in others... for no one has achieved true righteousness..."* [The "Luminous" Religion]

Consistent with these messages, Jesus preached – *"Forgive, always forgive"* [The "Luminous" Religion]

The Light 24:22 *"...[Y]ou should forgive and overlook..."* [Islam]

"God created a hundred portions of mercy. He placed one portion between His creation [so] they [could] have compassion on each other..." [Islam:

Saheeh Al-Bukhari, Saheeh Muslim, Al-Tirmidhi, et al.]

"To understand all is to forgive all."[75] [Sufism]

The point is we should not condemn another since none of us are without fault or sin. It is precisely for this reason that God constantly forgives, provides each of us with an individualized plan for salvation and offered Himself as the Universal Savior.

He knew our every imperfection before we were born – *"Before I formed you in the womb I knew you"* [Jeremiah 1:5] – still loved us enough to create us, and sought to remedy our flaws through *agape* love.

Universal Savior:

"[J]ust as one trespass resulted in condemnation for all... so also one righteous act resulted in... life for all..." [Romans 5:18]

Jesus, the Christ (c. 5 BCE-33 CE) is the Universal Savior and his salvation is universal. "The transformational events of [his] birth, life, death," and resurrection have, continue to, and will "impact all individuals" past, present, and future "regardless of their awareness of those events... [or if] one

33

'knows' him or not."[76] He is the Universal Savior who freely offered his life to fulfill the very meaning and depth of God's *agape* love such that the love of none other would or could surpass it.

Consequently each and every person involved in the events of his life and crucifixion are free of culpability and saved. Per French philosopher and theologian Jacques Ellul (1912-1994 CE), "It is inconceivable that the God who gives Himself in His Son to save us, should have created some people ordained to evil and damnation. There can only be one predestination to salvation. In and through Jesus Christ all people are predestined to be saved..."[77]

Had there been no one to carry out the crucifixion, God's mission could not have been accomplished and prophesy, namely Isaiah regarding the "Suffering Messiah" (written between 750-700 BCE) – *"[H]e took up our pain and bore our suffering... [H]e was pierced for our transgressions, he was crushed for our iniquities... [B]y his wounds we are healed... [H]e... made intercession for the transgressors."* [Isaiah 53:4-5, 12] – would not have been fulfilled.

Jesus also made it clear – no one was to blame – *"I am the good shepherd... I lay down my life for the sheep… No one takes it from me, but I lay it down of my own accord."* [John 10: 14-15 and 18]

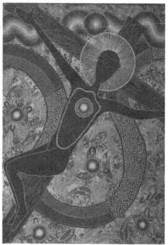

The Universal Savior depicted In *The Twelfth Station* by Aboriginal Artist Richard Campbell (b. 1956- CE)

Per Russian writer Fyodor Dostoyevsky (1821-1881 CE), "[Jesus] did this because of God's love for us and because of his love and obedience to… his Father. We're mistaken when we think it is… not the love of God, that brought Jesus to [the crucifixion, in which he bore] the consequence of our sins."[78]

Consistent with the Universal Savior laying down His life, He also raised it up in the resurrection through *agape* love – *"...I lay down my life – only to take it up again."* [John 10:17] During his 2007 CE Easter Vigil homily, Pope Benedict XVI (1927- CE) declared that the key that had opened the "gates of death" was Christ's cross of "radical love" because *"love is stronger than death"*[79] [Song of Songs 8:6] and unlimited in its possibilities.

"Nothing, not even death, can separate us from the love of God," [Romans 8:38-39] which, since it is imperishable, all-consuming, and unlimited in its possibilities, "makes it possible [for God] to [purify] and transform everyone" dead or alive since He "will not be content until the last precious soul has entered heaven"[80] so that His *agape* love retains perfection – "And God said to the soul: I desired you before the world began. I desire you now as you desire [M]e. And where the desires of two come together, there love is perfected."[81] [Mechtild of Magdeburg (1207-c. 1282/1294 CE)]

"To love is the road to strength. To love in spite of all is the secret of greatness..." L. Ron Hubbard (1911-1986 CE), founder of Scientology stated. This is the reason for the greatness of the cross and the resurrection's omnipotence that initiated universal salvation.

"Everything comes from love; all is ordained for the salvation of man. God does nothing without this goal in mind." [St. Catherine of Siena (1347-1380 CE)]

Christ's universal status has been affirmed not only by Christianity, but just about every major religion including but not limited to Judaism, Islam, Hinduism and Buddhism. This is not surprising since God offered Himself as the Universal Savior to fulfill His love for every living being past, present, and future. Per St. Justin Martyr (100-165 CE), "Christ is the Word of whom every race... [are] partakers." Accordingly Dutch theologian Desiderius Erasmus (1466-1536 CE) wrote, "Christ is more widespread than we understand."

And it is because of Christ that "many distinct paths, while remaining distinct, can lead to salvation."[82]

"I take this suffering upon myself provided that not one person... shall perish..." [Judaism – Pesikta Rabbati, Piska 36.1; Zohar II. 212a]

"[The Messiah], 'the raft of salvation and compassion,' suffered terrible woes so that all should be freed from karma. All of us are saved by his works..." [The "Luminous" Religion]

[54] *"He who is of [God]...* [71] *[the] Lord that was made flesh...* [54] *ordain[ed] that His saving grace should be made manifest.* [126] *...[T]hrough [Him] we attain... the final deliverance that destroyed... sin."*[83] [Buddhism]

"After creating the sky, waters, and the earth... the Lord almighty thought, 'I created the worlds. Now to provide for and to save these worlds I have to [send] a savior.' Thinking thus He gave birth to a man of Himself... When we were perishing, [God] came to save us by offering... [H]is own body on our behalf."[84] [Hinduism]

Marium 19:33-34 *"And peace on me on the day I was born, and on the day I die, and on the day I am raised to life. Such is Isa, son of Marium...* The Ranks [61:12] *He will forgive you your faults and cause you to enter into gardens, beneath, which rivers flow, and goodly dwellings in gardens of perpetuity..."* [Islam]

[2806] *"We were to have died,* [2807] *We were to have been lost...* [4256-4257] *[He] Descended, Ascended...* [4263] *Because of this not we died...* [4477] *Dead now therefore... death."*[85] [Mayan Religion]

Based on the above scriptures it is clear that the Universal Savior's crucifixion and resurrection are redemptive for everyone regardless of their religious beliefs. The cross and resurrection have given rebirth to each and every person in fulfillment of John 3:7 – *"You must be born again."* Through this rebirth, all are enabled to pass through the *"eye of the needle"* [Matthew 19:24] onto universal salvation since through the Universal Savior's blood, *"all things have become new."* [2 Corinthians 5:17]

Per German theologian Karl Rahner (1904-1984 CE), "Just as adherents to pre-Christian Judaism were able... to enter God's presence, so too, is it possible for adherents of other religions to enter [His] presence."[86]

This is the reason it is written in John 10:16 – *"And other sheep I have which are not of this fold; them also I must bring, and they will hear my voice; and there will be one flock and one shepherd."*

Consequently, it is written in Luke 13:29 – *"They shall come from the east, and from the west, and from the north, and from the south, and shall sit down in the kingdom of God"* and Revelation 7:9 – *"John got a glimpse into heaven and there he saw the heavenly multitude from all nations, kindred, people, and tongues."*

And if this is not enough, the Gnostic gospels also affirm universal salvation – *"He labored even on the Sabbath for the sheep which [had] fallen into the pit. He saved the life of that sheep... He... anoint[ed] [it] with [his blood]... He [did] the will of the One who called him... Each one's name comes to him."* [Gospel of Truth] *"We are saved. We have received salvation from end to end."* [The Treatise on the Resurrection ("The Letter to Rheginos")]

With this said, one caveat remains – God does not impose Himself upon us. This too is out of love. Per Rabbi Gershon Winkler, God's love "entails selfless gifting... not only of [Him]self, but also [in] stepping back... by withdrawal... to enable the other to emerge... exist [and] flourish."[87] In fact, He "guards our freedom,"[88] having granted us inalienable rights (e.g. right to life, liberty, and pursuit of happiness, which includes "freedom of religion" that helps shape and define our individual relationship with God).

"[The] conscience of man is sacred and to be respected..."[89] [Bahai'ism: Abdu'l-Bahá]

The Cow 2:256 *"There is no compulsion in religion..."* [Islam]

Because of this, St. Francis of Assisi (1182-1226 CE) wrote, "So precious is a person's faith in God, so precious; never should we harm that. Because He (God) gave birth to all religions."[90]

God gave each of us individuality and free will since "without an ability to choose, we cannot come to love…"[91] nor know and appreciate His love.

As we are in the image of God Who is love, we are called to reflect His love to the best of our ability as we exercise our freedom.

"Our purpose here is to observe, to learn, to grow, to love…"[92] [Aboriginal]

"God is love. Therefore love. Without distinction, without calculation, without procrastination, love." [Henry Drummond, Scottish Evangelist (1851-1897 CE)]

Love also, because a life without love is empty and wasted. Only love can provide enrichment and worth to the purpose of our lives.

At the same time, it is up to each of us to choose to accept God's love so that we can live eternally in His loving presence, known as "heaven," (*"[T]o be one with God"[93]* [Confucianism]) which is the opposite of Hell or the perception of the absence of His loving presence, the latter which despite prevailing views that date back to the Fifth Ecumenical Council (553 CE), is temporary rather than eternal based on preceding universalist teachings incorporated by St. Clement of Alexandria (c. 150-215 CE) and his pupil, Origen (185-254 CE) "that sinful and alienated souls – because of divine love and mercy – will ultimately be reconciled to God"[94] and the facts that *"God is love"* [1 John 4:8 and 16], His "love... is given without any regard for our goodness,"[95] and *"[W]ith [Him] all things are possible."* [Matthew 19:26]

Accordingly, Gregory of Nyssa (c. 335-395 CE), in his book *Sermo Catecheticus Magnus*, described: "The annihilation of evil, the restitution of all things, and the final restoration of evil men and evil spirits to the blessedness of union with God, so that He may be 'all in all,' embracing all things endowed with sense and reason."[96]

When accepting God's love, we must strive to follow His simple laws – love and forgive, which is facilitated if we allow Him to reside in our hearts. Optimally, we must also ask His forgiveness for our shortcomings as we make a sincere effort to do better – a process akin to metamorphisis. Setbacks are okay too as long as our efforts to improve are sincere since God already knows we are not perfect. Rabbi Brad Hirschfield's statement – "Rosh HaShanah is based not only on the availability of second chances, but also on the radical claim that each of us deserves a second chance, even if it's our hundredth one!"[97] – attests to this, illustrating the depth of God's *agape* love, "which never gives up [on us] and never withholds forgiveness."[98] This is so, because *"God is love"* [1 John 4:8 and 16] and "[l]ove is an act of endless forgiveness," per Canadian philosopher Jan Vanier (1928- CE).

Furthermore, since "God's love knows no bounds, even those who do not seek forgiveness may [still] be forgiven" based on Hindu Sura 51:19 and Matthew 6:8, respectively – *"True charity remembers not only those in need who ask, but also those who are prevented for some reason from asking"*[99] and *"…[Y]our Father knows what you need before you ask [H]im."*

God's love is that great!

After all, God is our Father Who loves us unconditionally and even though He may discipline us at times, His divine punishment is not without end and it is redemptive in nature. It "is based

43

William Sutherland

[solely] on giving a person what he or she needs rather than deserves."[100]

"The Lord disciplines those [H]e loves..." [Hebrews 12:6] and since God's *agape* love is "intense... [it] does not measure... it just gives." [Blessed Mother Teresa (1910-1997 CE)]

"Praise the Lord... [W]ho forgives all your sins... [W]ho redeems your life from the pit... [H]e does not treat us as our sins deserve or repay us according to our iniquities. For as high as the heavens are above the earth, so great is [H]is love." [Psalm 103:2-4 and 10-11]

"...[B]ehold, the Lord hath redeemed my soul from hell... and I am encircled about eternally in the arms of [H]is love." [The Church of Jesus Christ of Latter-Day Saints: 2 Nephi 1:15]

"...[T]he arm of the LORD is not too short to save..." [Isaiah 59:1]

These passages and Blessed Mother Teresa's statement lend further credence to the universalist view that hell is temporary. Eternal damnation, even if one is deserving of it from a human perspective, certainly is not what a person needs or desires nor redemptive in nature. In addition, God

44

knows better what we need than we do (especially when irrational thoughts and mental illness are considered) such that out of His *agape* love He may guide us back into alignment with our needs when we stray from our best interests.

Out of *agape* love, *"God is our God for ever and ever; [H]e will be our guide even to the end."* [Psalm 48:14] Consequently, *"[e]ven though I walk through the valley of the shadow of death, I will fear no evil, for [Y]ou are with me; [Y]our rod and [Y]our staff, they comfort me."* [Psalm 23:4]

"...His Protecting Hand is over all." [Sikhism – Sri Guru Granth Sahib] Thus, "[a]s long as I breathe, I hope" [Latin Proverb] because of God's *agape* love.

Therefore, in the words of Gregory of Nyssa, it is possible that "when death approaches to life, and darkness to light, and the corruptible to the incorruptible, the inferior is done away with and reduced to non-existence, and the thing purged is benefited, just as the dross is purged from gold by fire. In the same way... when the evil of nature... has been taken away, whensoever the restoration to their old condition of the things that now lie in wickness takes place, there will be a unanimous thanksgiving from the whole creation, both of those

45

who have been punished in the purification and of those who have not at all needed purification."[101]

Perhaps Sufi poet Rūmī was describing this very process when he wrote of God whom He called "Love" – "...He has annihilated me and filled me only with Him. His fire has penetrated all the atoms of my body. Of 'me' only my name remains; the rest is Him."[102]

"God is a consuming fire." [Hebrews 12:29]

To extrapolate based on the above passage from Hebrews 12:29 and the fact that *"God is love"* [1 John 4:8 and 16], the fire Gregory of Nyssa and Rūmī refer to can only be "Love." Thus this purifying fire does not harm or destroy since such a result would be the antithesis or opposite of love, which is God's very Being. This is not only possible but has been demonstrated through the burning bush. Though on fire, it was not harmed when God appeared to Moses in Exodus 3.

Instead, to use the words of St. Thomas Aquinas, this fire, which is love merely "perfects and purifies."[103] This does not mean, though, that the experience will be pleasant.

At the same time, the purifying fire does not purge individuality. Per Hindu poet Tukaram (1577-1650 CE), *Can water drink itself?* – "The [individual]... must remain distinct from [God]. Only thus will he come to know God's joyful love."[104]

Had this not been the case, there would not have been a purpose for creation since it would have been sufficient for God to love Himself and know and appreciate His love solely through Himself, which in reality is the ultimate and complete selfish and narcissistic opposite of His very being!

"O Living Flame of Love... [h]ow gently... how lovingly [and] [h]ow tenderly [Y]ou fill me with love."[105] [St. John of the Cross (1542-1591 CE)]

"Let us not be in doubt... concerning the hope of our salvation, see that He who bore sufferings for our sakes is very concerned for our salvation; His mercifulness is far more extensive than we can conceive, His grace is greater than what we ask for... [because] human sin is infinitely small in comparison with the infinite mercy of God"[106] such that "no one is beyond the possibility of salvation."[107]

Thus per Pope (St.) John Paul II, based on Revelation 19:13 – "Christ... for ever *'clad in a robe dipped in blood"* is "the everlasting, invincible guarantee of universal salvation."[108]

Accordingly, Scottish minister Oswald Chambers (1874-1917 CE) wrote in the essay, *It is Finished* – "The cross of Christ means that the salvation of God goes deeper down than the deepest depths of iniquity man can commit. No person can get beyond the reach of Jesus; He made a way back to the throne of God from the very heart of hell by His tremendous atonement."[109]

This is forever demonstrated through the "Washing of Feet" by the Universal Savior as recounted by Congregational minister George Marion McClellan (1860-1934 CE):

Christ washed the feet of Judas! Christ knew the whole, [a]nd still in love he stooped and washed his feet... [S]o ineffable his love... [t]hat pity fill his great forgiving heart...

Christ washed the feet of Judas! And thus a girded servant, self-abased, [t]aught that no wrong this side the gate of heaven [w]as ever too great to wholly be effaced, [a]nd though unasked, in spirit be forgiven.[110]

"Washing of Feet"
[John 13: 1-16]

Furthermore, since the concept of eternal damnation is incompatible with God's unfailing *agape* love, the Greek word *aionios* "indefinite but limited duration" vs. *aidios* "perpetual" was used when referring to hell in early New Testament writings,[111] as well as the fact that the idea of eternal damnation emerged some 350 years after universalist thoughts had comprised the foundation of early Christianity, it is not only possible but likely that universal salvation is the accurate theology of God Who is love.

Where God is, there is love. Where there is love, there is mercy.

"[T]he Lord is so kind that... He always remains with the [creation]." [Hinduism: Srimad-Bhagavatam 3:26:16]

49

"[Whithersoever you turn, there is the Face of God."[112] [Sufism: Muhyiddin Ibn Arabi (1165-1240 CE)]

"If I go up to the heavens, you are there; if I make my bed in Sheol (hell), [Y]ou are there." [Psalm 139:8]

"The love of God is greater far [t]han tongue or pen can ever tell; It goes beyond the highest star, [a]nd reaches to the lowest hell..."[113] [Frederick M. Lehman (1868-1953 CE)]

God's love is so great that it is even evident in His anger and wrath. However, even though many mistakenly base God's anger and wrath on human conceptions and equate them to human emotions, they are "very different from human [anger and] wrath."[114]

First, God's anger and wrath never relinquish love even at their height because *"God's love never fails."* [Psalm 136:1]

Second, God's anger and wrath are not vindictive. Rather, they are redemptive and forgiving.

Third, God's anger and wrath are directed solely against evil and not creation. God hates evil and injustice because they are the antitheses or opposite of His very Being of love and violate His simple commandments that as mentioned earlier, can be fulfilled simply through love. God does not and never will hate a single being of His creation.

Consequently, even though Reformed Church revivalist Jonathan Edwards (1703-1758 CE), in his fiery 1741 CE sermon, *Sinners in the [H]ands of an angry God*, in all probability did not consciously plan it, God's loving mercy still emerged through his words – "His wrath... burns like a fire; He looks upon you as worthy of nothing else, but to be cast into the fire... You have offended [H]im infinitely more than ever a stubborn rebel did his prince. And yet it is nothing but [H]is hand that holds you from falling into the fire..."[115]

God's love is that great!

"For when You behold us in our pitiable condition, we feel the effect of Your mercy... You save us miserable creatures and spare us..."[116] [St. Anselm of Canterbury (1033-1109 CE)]

The anger and wrath of God Who is *"slow to anger [and] abounding in love"* [Numbers 14:18] are transient and passing. They last but for a moment and most importantly, as illustrated in Reverend

William Sutherland

Edwards' above sermon, remain subject to love. Nothing can supercede nor overpower divine love based on Psalm 136:1 since *"God is love."* [1 John 4:8 and 16]

"You do not stay angry forever but delight to show mercy." [Micah 7:18]

"[T]he Lord will turn from [H]is... anger, will show you mercy, and will have compassion on you." [Deuteronomy 13:17]

Per Dennis Ngien, professor of Systematic Theology at Tyndale University College & Seminary, Toronto, Canada, God's anger and wrath are "expression[s] of pure love that [do] not allow [H]im to stand by idly in the face of [evil and injustice]." They are expressions of "active love... which opposes anything that stands between [Him] and us... proof that [H]e cares"[117] for and loves each and every one of us.

It is out of *agape* love, God must save that *"one lost sheep"* [Luke 15:4-7] and *"draw all to Himself."* [John 12:32] God loves each of us to such a degree that He views "the [L]over and the beloved [as] one and inseparable"[118] such that He will not be satisfied until all are united with Him in paradise.

52

"Nothing will be able to part us. The flame of Your love will never die."[119]

"*Suppose one of you has a hundred sheep and loses one of them. Doesn't he leave the ninety-nine... and go after the lost sheep until he finds it? And when he finds it, he joyfully puts it on his shoulders and goes home. Then he... says, 'Rejoice with me; I have found my lost sheep.' I tell you that in the same way there will be more rejoicing in heaven over one sinner who repents than over ninety-nine righteous persons who do not need to repent.*" [Luke 15:4-7]

But why reject God's *agape* love when His commandments are simple to follow and love is not only good for the spiritual part of our existence, but also the physical and psychological through alleviation of "negative emotional states, increased self-esteem,"[120] and lowered stress levels, to name just a few of the benefits?

Basically, it can be said that aside from love as called for by God, everything else in comparison is of little importance. Per Edith Stein (1891-1942 CE), "All that we do is a means to an end, but love is an end in itself, because God is love."[121] In other words, we are one with God when we reciprocate His love because He is not a means to an end but the end Itself as revealed by Psalm 73:25-26 – *"Whom have I in heaven but [Y]ou? And earth has nothing I desire besides [Y]ou... God is the strength of my heart and my portion forever."*

Consequently, even though God does not spare the rod, He does not use it to inflict unnecessary pain that would leave physical, psychological, and spiritual scars since that would be abuse and "love binds and builds, heals and hallows, [and] redeems and restores."[122] Rather, He uses it as a staff to guide us so that we can maximize our spiritual growth. "[He] shows mercy, compassion, and justice to all."[123] [Judaism]

"The Lord says: 'Come then, come back to me, and come to know me as a father; for see, I return good for evil, love for injuries, and for deep wounds a deeper love,'" St. Peter Chrysologus (c. 380-450 CE) wrote of God's loving call.[124] The Universal Savior epitomized St. Peter Chrysologus' words. He was willing to suffer greatly, he loved his enemies and he forgave all who inflicted iniquities upon him – *"Father, forgive them..."* [Luke 23:34]

Per Origen, *The Words of Christ* (250 CE), these three words that emanated out of God's love are so powerful, "[t]he result... will only be fully known at the last day, when their greatness will be made manifest to all..."

Why? Because these three words are timeless and unlimited in context. They were, are, and always will be directed towards each and every being of creation, past, present, and future without exception!

In the meantime, we can get a superficial understanding of Origen's statement through the words of St. Thérèse of Lisieux (1873-1897 CE), "[E]very soul will find forgiveness." Even those who completely reject God will be forgiven since in the timeless words of Luke 23:34 – *"they do not know what they are doing."*

Consequently, when St. John of the Cross asked God in a mystical conversation – "Is [it] the fate of any heart to not reach [Y]ou?" – He answered, "No, no that is not the fate of any soul... I want all souls to consummate with [M]e."[125] God's love is that great!

Last, as mentioned earlier, since heaven is free of the stain of sin, and God will not allow it to enter, He renews all of creation – *"'Behold,' says the Lord. 'I make all things new.'"* [Revelation 21:5]

We are all purified by the Universal Savior's blood –
*"[T]hey have washed their robes and made them
white in the blood of the Lamb."* [Revelation 7:14]

*"The Lord... dyes us in the color of His Love... [He] is
the Purifier of sinners."* [Sikhism – Sri Guru Granth
Sahib]

"Blessed [are those]... whose sin is covered."
[Psalm 32:1]

Why? Because "God's faithful love will never
lessen and will never abandon us... [not even to]
death" or hell, the latter based on His loving
presence as mentioned in Psalm 139:8.[126]

Accordingly, because of His *agape* love, the finite
nature of hell and the reality of universal salvation
are affirmed in Psalm 145:9-11: *"The Lord is good
to all; [H]e has compassion on all [H]e has made.
All [Y]our works... tell of the glory of [Y]our
kingdom."* If damnation was eternal and salvation
was limited, how could *all* of God's creation be able
to experience and tell of the glory of His kingdom?

Consistent with this, the concept of karma
(espoused by Eastern religions that predate
Abrahamic faiths) entails different stages of
renewal, in which the God of Love can intervene to

God is Love

improve one's karma to expedite the process of attaining nirvana (salvation).

"[K]arma is not eternal..." since *"the Lord is very affectionate to... living entities..."* [Hinduism: Bhagavad-gita, Introduction and Srimad-Bhagavatam 3:26:16]

In Zoroastrianism, "everyone eventually leaves... hell" when they "are purified [to] join the righteous [with] [G]od."[127]

At the same time, even though early Judaism "had no concept of hell... [t]he overwhelming majority of rabbinic thought accepts its concept but maintains that people are not in [hell] forever... The gates of *teshuva* (return) are said to be always open... so one can align [their] will with that of God at any moment"[128] to enter into His loving presence.

This is corroborated by the Kabbalah, in which "the concept of everlasting damnation... doesn't exist [since] we are finite and our sins are finite [such that] our punishment or atonement must be finite..."[129] According to Rabbi Max Weiman, at the end of time, if it takes that long, "the entire creation [will be] corrected and rectified."[130]

Per Rob Bell (b. 1970 CE), *Love Wins* (HarperOne, New York, 2011 CE), "God has inaugurated a movement in Jesus' resurrection to renew, restore, and reconcile everything."[131]

This is because, God's "deepest nature is... love" and His "will that all... be restored to Him is predestined absolutely... He has elected all... to salvation."[132] [Unification Church] *"[O]ur citizenship is in heaven."* [Philippians 3:20]

The Companions 39:53 *"Despair not of the Mercy of God; for God forgives all sins, for He is Oft-Forgiving, Most-Merciful."* [Islam] *"Indeed, My mercy supercedes [M]y punishment."* [Islam: Saheeh Al-Bukhari, Saheeh Muslim]

Accordingly, the words in Irving Karchmar's novel, *Master of the Jinn: A Sufi Novel* (CreateSpace, Charleston, SC, 2004 CE) that portrays modern Sufi mysticism, accurately depicts God when He says, "[F]ear not. For thou canst not fall so low that I cannot raise thee up."[133] [Sufism]

All of this is possible because "God's love is greater and better than our minds can imagine... He has chosen us from the beginning to be saved... [because He] loves every person... with the same

degree of love. God loves everyone equally...
[His] love is for everyone."[134]

"The Lord God is... the Lover of [all]." [Sikhism – Sri
Guru Granth Sahib][135] and nothing can "prevent
[Him] from loving all His children."[136]

"My child, I love you... No matter what you say or
do... You don't have to do anything... Whatever
you do in life... I'll still love you... My love for you
doesn't change. It was, is, and will always be..."[137]

God's love is that great!

*"...[S]uppose a woman has ten silver coins and
loses one. Doesn't she light a lamp, sweep the
house and search carefully until she finds it? And
when she finds it, she... says, 'Rejoice with me; I
have found my lost coin.' In the same way... there
is rejoicing in the presence of the angels of God
over one sinner who repents."* [Luke 15:8-10]

We are worth that much to God that He will search
for and seek each of us until we are found! It does
not matter what one has done or how far we have
strayed. God's love will not allow Him to rest until
He finds us so that our individual heavenly
inheritence does not go unclaimed!

Per Pope (St.) John Paul II, "There is no one who cannot discover and find a place in God's love... There exists no one so bad, so brought down, so broken down, that [they] cannot find a place in that love... [He] loves us not because we have merited it or are worthy of it; rather God's love for us is freely given and unearned, surpassing all we could ever hope for or imagine."[138]

In the words of German monk Martin Luther (1483-1586 CE), founder of the Lutheran Church, "neither prophet, nor apostle, nor angel was ever able fully to express and... no heart [able to] fathom or marvel at... the goodness of God,"[139] which is His *agape* love. God's *agape* love is so great, it even loves the unlovable!

Why? Because in the words of Dieter F. Uchtdorf (1940- CE), German aviator, author, and Counselor in the First Presidency of The Church of Jesus Christ of Latter-Day Saints, "God's love encompasses us completely... Though we are incomplete, God loves us completely. Though we are imperfect, God loves us perfectly."[140]

For God, Who is Love, this is characteristically simple based on the words of John Winthrop (1588-1649 CE), a Puritan lawyer and a leading figure in the founding of Massachusetts Colony, "Love is the bond of perfection."[141]

In addition, because of the great depth and infinite, eternal and profound nature of God's love, St. Catherine of Siena wrote, "You [God], deep well of love, it seems you are so madly in love with your creatures that you could not live without us!"[142]

At the same time, because of God's great love and seeming inability to live without His creation, St. Francis of Assisi wrote, "I have come to learn: God adores His creation."[143] To God, we are truly precious and worthy of veneration! To God we are truly deserving of eternal existence!

His love is that great!

Therefore, even though no thought, word, deed, or act can repay God for His *agape* love, out of gratitude we can seek to follow His simple laws and even rejoice in adversity and suffering (filled with love, proclaiming, "If not I, then who? Better I than another!") since such adversity and suffering enables us to beatifically unify our pain with that of the Universal Savior enroute to our eschatological resurrection, all because *"The Lord is full of compassion and mercy."* [James 5:11] He is [The Opening 1:2] *"the Merciful, the Compassionate."* [Islam]

William Sutherland

Indeed, *"God is love"* [1 John 4:8 and 16] and He "loves each of us as if there were only one of us to love."[144] [St. Augustine]

Accordingly, God's love, which is intensely personal declares, "I will first of all love you!"[145] [Unification Church]

In fact, God's love is so intensely personal, He declares, "My name is not complete without yours... I am made whole by your life."[146] [Sufism: Shams-ud-din Muhammad Hafiz (c. 1320-1389 CE)]

And God loves each of us for who we are rather than by human standards such as appearance, conformity, or what others expect us to be. It does not matter if one is disabled either. God already knows everything about us and there is nothing someone can tell Him that He does not already know that would or even could cause Him to withdraw His love. *"Nothing in all creation is hidden from God... Everything is... laid bare before the eyes of Him..."* [Hebrews 4:13]

In fact, "everything He knows calls forth more love."[147] This is an irrefutable, infallible fact since *"[t]he Lord chose you because He loved you"* [Deuteronomy 7:8] and always will love you!

God is Love

In the eyes of God, He did not make a mistake when He created you. He knew exactly what He was doing! "I made you, dear, and all I make is perfect."[148] Accordingly one may only conclude, "there [is] a place [in life] for me [and a place in God's loving plan of salvation for me!]"[149]

And so even if one is unjustly stripped of worth and unfairly condemned or rejected, God's love for that individual is not reduced or eliminated. Instead, it is strengthened.

It is in this context that Jesus reached out, touched and healed a leper [Matthew 8:2-3], defended the adulterous woman whom society wanted to stone [John 8:3-11], and dined with social outcasts such as the tax collector [Mark 2:15-17].

In the 21st century, Jesus would undoubtedly reach out, touch and heal one suffering from AIDS, accept and forgive the woman who had an abortion, and dine with members of the LGBT community, prostitutes, the incarcerated and the so-called "unsaved." And in future ages, he would reach out, touch and heal one suffering from some new, stigmatizing disease, forgive one of some other en vogue "condemning" sin of the day, and dine with those disenfranchised from and

63

marginalized by the mainstream society of that respective period.

And when critics would complain or condemn, Jesus would surely answer, *"What is that to you!"* [John 21:22] He would not allow them to adversely influence his and thus God's love because no person or entity has the right to dictate whom God should love!

It is in this setting, one can hear God's resounding declaration – "I also love those who most need My love!"

Accordingly, God's love is not based on what society and/or others may think of you! It does not matter who you are! No person (not even you yourself!) or establishment can keep God from loving you!

"[N]either... angels nor demons... nor any powers... nor anything else... will be able to separate us from the love of God." [Romans 8:38-39]

"I am filled with love for you."[150] [Tenrikyo: Sacred Book 8-60]

God is Love

God's love cannot be limited by "who we are,"[151] human feelings, thoughts, perceptions, personal experiences, and cultural values.

Thus, God's *agape* love is unhindered by human judgment even when it appears the latter limits the former. Therefore, when burdened or rejected, despair not. The Universal Savior is "aware of your rejection... He identifies with your hurt [and]... will bring you comfort... [f]or [h]e too – was rejected."[152] *"He was despised and rejected by mankind... and we held him in low esteem."* [Isaiah 53:3]

"God [through love]... sees every unseen wound [and] mends every unbearable pain."[153]

It is because of this, Philoxenus of Mabbug (c. 440-523 CE), a bishop in the Syrian monophysite church "exhort[ed]... early monks... to treat one another with the gentleness of God, [W]ho especially loves the ones the world despises..."[154]

Per 1 Peter 2:3 you are *"a precious, living stone in the eyes of God."*[155]

Therefore instead of lamenting, "[t]hink of the purest, most all-consuming love you can imagine... [M]ultiply that love by an infinite amount – [and] that is the measure of God's love for you."[156]

65

And if this is not enough, think of God's indubitable response to the question – "Do You love me?" – "I love you so much, I died for you!"

Because of this in the words of Mary Baker Eddy (1821-1910 CE), founder of Christian Science, "Fed by Thy love divine we live, [f]or [l]ove alone is [l]ife."[157]

"The Eternal... made all things in [l]ove. On [l]ove they all depend." [Farid ud Din Attar, 12th Century CE Sufi poet]

"You are... kept in being by My [l]ove."[158]

Best yet, God will never cease loving us – *"I have loved you with an everlasting love..."* [Jeremiah 31:3] Thus, by the definition of God's love, which we know to be everlasting, we are ensured eternal life since divine love alone is life itself! Thus our lives will not be extinguished even when we pass from this earth! Therefore, as each of us was "[l]oved into being"[159] and is sustained by love, each of us will be loved into eternity!

As a result, God's love is reassuring and comforting since passing on is simply moving from one existence to another. It is not the end of our existence into eternal nothingness! Only a catastrophic failure in God's love would render the latter possible. However, since God's love is perfect and never ceases, such a catastrophic failure can never occur!

In fact, so great is the depth of God's love that words and thoughts cannot adequately describe it, images cannot sufficiently depict it, wisdom and understanding cannot fully fathom or comprehend it and all the religions in the universes combined cannot even marginally proclaim it. With this in mind we need not attempt to fully discern it.

Instead, all we need to know is simply *"God is love"* [1 John 4:8 and 16] and this should suffice, inspiring us to love both Him Who created and saved us, and all His creation, making our temporary abode a better place as we await our call to eternity in His loving presence.

At the same time, we should refrain from attempting to assign eternal destiny to another. We must not act like the self-righteous man who prayed, *"I thank you that I am not like other people – robbers, evildoers, adulterers – or even like this tax collector. I fast twice a week and give a tenth of all I get"* [Luke 18:11] – since we are saved solely by God's love rather than by works as stated in Ephesians 2:8-9. Nor should we begrudge the "wages" of another as recounted in the *Parable of the Workers in the Vineyard* [Matthew 20: 1-16] in which every laborer (those hired first and those hired last) was paid the same, identical wage. In fact, it would not have mattered if the laborer had been hired at all – he or she would have still been given the same, identical wage!

Why? "[B]ecause it is God alone [W]ho sees the whole of who we are... [W]ho understands the depths of our temptations and the extent of our sufferings."[160] It is precisely for this reason the Universal Savior declared, *"I have not come to call the righteous, but sinners"* [Mark 2:17] giving hope to each and every one of us!

Thus, debating the concept of universal salvation serves no useful purpose and provides no spiritual benefit. Instead, we should just open our hearts and embrace God's unconditional *agape* love for what it is with the same simple acceptance as Evangelical writer Rachel Evans (1981- CE) – "I don't know all the details of how love will prevail... but I believe that it will."[161]

Consequently the following question is of universal importance and applicable to each and every person, past, present and future: "If *I* in my wretched state can be renewed through the

Universal Savior's shed blood simply because *'God is love'* [1 John 4:8 and 16], who am *I* to assign condemnation to or to begrudge the salvation of another?"

At the same time, we should ask – "How am I any more worthy of salvation than another?" – with full knowledge that no one is deserving of this priceless gift of God – not even the greatest of the saints! With this in mind, universalism is the only possible equitable solution to our salvific predicament. Therefore we can only gain individual salvation because it is universal in scope thanks to God's *agape* love!

In this context, I quote evangelist Angella Sutherland (1971- CE) with regard to God's salvific love – "I love You and only want to live for You... [for] who am I that You are so merciful to me!"

Accordingly, we should praise God with the following words – "It is simply because You are love that I am saved!"

In fact, God's love is so profound, it does not matter if one's body is destroyed by disease, murder or suicide, or a fetus by miscarriage or abortion – salvation is for all! Every conceived being – past, present, and future – born and unborn alike is eternally embraced by divine love and saved!

"My God, who can have tasted the sweetness of [Your] love, then wanted another in place of [You]?" [Islam: Supplication 77][162]

"May your roots go down deep into the soil of God's marvelous love. And may you have the power to understand... how wide, how long, how high, and how deep His love really is." [Ephesians 3:17-18]

And may you know no matter who you are, what you are, what you have done, what you have not done, and/or how lonely, abandoned, rejected or even condemned you may feel – you are loved and always will be!

"God is Love"
1 John 4: 8 and 16

---

[1] William Sutherland. Unum. Trafford Publishing. USA. 2012. p.188.

[2] Bronwen Henry. God. Love. Kindness. And World Religions. Connection. 2012. Issue 1. p. 12.

[3] 20 Inspirational Bible Verses About God's Love. 11 September 2011. http://www.whatchristianswanttoknow.com/20-inspirational-bible-verses-about-gods-love/

[4] Matthew Weinberg. The Human Rights Discourse: A Bahá'í Perspective. Bahá'í Topics. 15 July 2013. http://info.bahai.org/article-1-8-3-2.html

[5] The Philosophy of Divine Love. 17 July 2013. http://www.divine-innocence.org/Philosophy%20of%20Divine%20Love.htm

[6] Bronwen Henry. God. Love. Kindness. And World Religions. Connection. 2012. Issue 1. p. 12.

[7] The New Church. Wikipedia.org. 13 September 2012. http://en.wikipedia.org/wiki/Swedenborgianism#Beliefs

[8] The New Church. Wikipedia.org. 13 September 2012. http://en.wikipedia.org/wiki/Swedenborgianism#Beliefs

[9] Bronwen Henry. God. Love. Kindness. And World Religions. Connection. 2012. Issue 1. p. 12.

[10] God Loves Us. Corpus Christi Parish.com. 16 September 2012.

William Sutherland

[11] What Does Judaism Say About Love? Moment. September/October 2010.

[12] Daniel Ladinsky. Love Poems from God: Twelve Sacred Voices from the East and West. 22 July 2013. http://www.poetseers.org/spiritual-and-devotional-poets/contemp/love-poems-from-god/mira/a-limb-just-moved/

[13] What Does Judaism Say About Love? Moment. September/October 2010.

[14] Love Divine, All Loves Excelling. Wikipedia.org. 27 May 2013. http://en.wikipedia.org/wiki/Love_Divine,_All_Loves_Excelling

[15] Lev Shestov. God is Love: Kierkegaard and the Existential Philosophy. 17 July 2013. http://www.angelfire.com/nb/shestov/sk/sk_16.html

[16] Plato (427-347 BCE). Internet Encyclopedia of Philosophy. 9 May 2009. http://www.iep.utm.edu/plato/

[17] Donagh O'Shea. The Madness of God. Goodnews.ie. 2009. http://www.goodnews.ie/jacobswellsdec.shtml

[18] Donagh O'Shea. The Madness of God. Goodnews.ie. 2009. http://www.goodnews.ie/jacobswellsdec.shtml

[19] Tzvi Freeman. Divine Madness. Chabad.org. 17 July 2013. http://www.chabad.org/library/article_cdo/aid/273242/jewish/Divine-Madness.htm

72

[20] William Shakespeare. Shakespeare Quotations on Love. 23 July 2013. http://www.shakespeare-online.com/quotes/shakespeareonlove.html

[21] William Sutherland. Unum. Trafford Publishing. USA. 2012. p. 170.

[22] God Loves Us. Corpus Christi Parish.com. 16 September 2012.

[23] Sir John Templeton. Agape Love. Templeton Foundation Press. Philadelphia, PA. 1999. pp. 1 and 4.

[24] Agape. Wikipedia. 7 August 2012.

[25] Love in Islam. Moral Stories, Narratives, Anecdotes, Prophet Stories, Short Stories, and More... 16 September 2012. http://www.ezsoftech.com/stories/love.in.islam.asp

[26] Comparing Eastern Views and Western Views. 16 September 2012. http://www.bnaiyer.com/Hindu-Special-Articles/s-comp-01.html

[27] Daniel Ladinsky. Love Poems from God: Twelve Sacred Voices from the East and West. Penguin Compass. New York. 2002. p. 5.

[28] Agape. Wikipedia. 7 August 2012.

[29] Ben Coblentz. Born to Love. TGS International. Berlin, OH. 1993.

[30] Job Hupton. The Love of God. 19 July 2013.
http://www.mountzionpbc.org/books/Job%20Hupton%20The%
20Love%20of%20God.htm

[31] Job Hupton. The Love of God. 19 July 2013.
http://www.mountzionpbc.org/books/Job%20Hupton%20The%
20Love%20of%20God.htm

[32] Kevin J. Vanhoozer. Nothing Greater, Nothing Better. Wm.
B. Eerdmans Publishing Co. Grand Rapids, MI. 2001. p. 8.

[33] Kevin J. Vanhoozer. Nothing Greater, Nothing Better. Wm.
B. Eerdmans Publishing Co. Grand Rapids, MI. 2001. p. 17.

[34] Arthur C. Clarke. Lonely Minds in the Universe. Springer.
New York, NY. 18 November 2007.

[35] Religion and Science. Stanford Encyclopedia of Philosophy.
2010. 16 April 2012. http://plato.stanford.edu/entries/religion-
science/#Con

[36] Margaret Murney Glenn. Christian Science: The Revelation
of Love as Divine Principle. 1 December 1933.
http://www.cslectures.org/Glenn/CS-
The%20Revelation%20of%20Love-Glenn.htm

[37] Sir John Templeton. Agape Love. Templeton Foundation
Press. Philadelphia, PA. 1999. p. 11.

[38] Emiel Van Den Boomen. Mesmerizing Vietnam – Fusion in
religion. 3 July 2011.
http://www.actoftraveling.com/2011/07/mesmerizing-about-
vietnam-fusion-in-religion/ and Basic Catechism of Caodaism.

8 March 2012. http://en.nhipcautamgiao.net/news/136-basic-catechism-of-caodaism-1.html

[39] Saman Suttam. Wikipedia.org. 29 July 2012. http://en.wikipedia.org/wiki/Saman_Suttam

[40] Unity in Diversity Quotes. 6 May 2011. http://dropsoul.com/mystic-quotes.php

[41] Mark Reynolds. In defense of religion. McGill News Alumni Magazine. Fall/Winter 2011. p. 11.

[42] William Sutherland. Unum. Trafford Publishing. USA. 2012. p. 170.

[43] Cheondoism. The Blaze.com. 18 September 2012. http://religions.theblaze.com/l/45/Cheondoism

[44] Within This Earthen Vessel. Poet Seers. 22 July 2013. http://www.poetseers.org/the-poetseers/kabir/kabir-index/within/

[45] God. Love. Kindness. And World Religions. Connection. 2012. Issue 1. p. 21.

[46] Love in Islam. Moral Stories, Narratives, Anecdotes, Prophet Stories, Short Stories, and More... 16 September 2012. http://www.ezsoftech.com/stories/love.in.islam.asp

[47] Mirabai Biography. Biography Online. 22 July 2013. http://www.biographyonline.net/spiritual/mirabai.html

[48] Love in Islam. Moral Stories, Narratives, Anecdotes, Prophet Stories, Short Stories, and More... 16 September 2012. http://www.ezsoftech.com/stories/love.in.islam.asp

[49] The World's Religions: Shintoism. 17 September 2012. http://theworldsreligions.com/shintoism

[50] Sir John Templeton. Agape Love. Templeton Foundation Press. Philadelphia, PA. 1999. p. 58.

[51] Sir John Templeton. Agape Love. Templeton Foundation Press. Philadelphia, PA. 1999. p. 10.

[52] Thomas Talbott. Universal Salvation. The Current Debate. 2004.

[53] Eric Reitan. Eternal damnation and blessed ignorance: is the damnation of some incompatible with the salvation of any? Cambridge University Press. Cambridge, UK. 2002. p. 430.

[54] Religious Diversity (Pluralism). Stanford Encyclopedia of Philosophy. 25 May 2004.

[55] Inclusivism. Wikipedia.Org. 13 July 2012.

[56] Seeking Answers: Questions about God and Life. Connection. 2008. Issue 4. p. 6.

[57] Sri Swami Sivananda. Shintoism. 20 February 2005. http://www.dlshq.org/religions/shintoism.htm

[58] Rābi'ah al-Basrī. My God and My Lord. 22 July 2013. http://poemhunter.com/poem/my-god-and-my-lord/

[59] Thomas Aquinas Quotes. BrainyQuote.com. 15 July 2013. http://www.brainyquote.com/quotes/authors/t/thomas_aquinas.html

[60] Daniel Ladinsky. Love Poems from God: Twelve Sacred Voices from the East and West. Penguin Compass. New York. 2002. p. 123.

[61] 20 Inspirational Bible Verses About God's Love. 11 September 2011. http://www.whatchristianswanttoknow.com/20-inspirational-bible-verses-about-gods-love/

[62] Patricia Ward Biederman. Cao Dai Fuses Great Faiths of the World. Los Angeles Times. 7 January 2006. http://articles.latimes.com/2006/jan/07/local/me-beliefs7

[63] Unitarian Universalist beliefs. Religious Tolerance.org. 21 July 2013. http://www.religioustolerance.org/u-u2.htm

[64] R.J. Zwi Werblowsky. Universal Religion and Universalist Religion. International Journal for Philosophy of Religion. Vol 2, No. 1. Spring 1971. p. 13.

[65] God. Love. Kindness. And World Religions. Connection. 17 July 2013. http://www.newchurch.org/connection/issues/god-is-not-only-christian/god-love-kindness.html

[66] Hindu Doctrine of Ahimsa.

[67] Thus Spake Lord Mahavir: Excerpts from the Sacred Books of Jainism. Jainism Literature Center. 21 July 2013.

http://www.fas.harvard.edu/~pluralsm/affiliates/jainism/quote/q
uote1.htm

[68] Unitarian Universalist beliefs. Religious Tolerance.org. 21
July 2013. http://www.religioustolerance.org/u-u2.htm

[69] Teresa of Ávila quotes. Goodreads.com. 21 July 2013.
http://www.goodreads.com/author/quotes/74226.Teresa_of_vil
a

[70] Mercy Amba Oduyoye. THE AFRICAN EXPERIENCE OF
GOD THROUGH THE EYES OF AN AKAN WOMAN. Cross
Currents. Vol. 47, Issue 4. Winter 1997-98.

[71] E.A. Wallis Budge. The Gods of the Egyptians. Dover
Publications. New York. 1969. p. 259 and Donald B. Redford,
Ed. The Oxford Guide: Essential Guide to Egyptian Mythology.
Berkley Publishing Group. New York. 2003. pp. 302-307.

[72] Sir John Templeton. Agape Love. Templeton Foundation
Press. Philadelphia, PA. 1999. p. 68.

[73] Llewellyn Vaughan-Lee. Love is a Fire: The Sufi's Mystical
Journey Home. The Golden Sufi Center. Inverness, CA.
2000. p. 7.

[74] Henry Stob. The Amazing Love of God. Perspectives: A
Journal of Reformed Thought. November 2003.
http://www.rca.org/page.aspx?pid=3248

[75] William Sutherland. Unum. Trafford Publishing. USA.
2012. p. 171.

[76] God. Love. Kindness. And World Religions. Connection. 2012. Issue 1. p. 15.

[77] Universalism Through Church History... Quotes. Tentmaker.com. 3 October 2012. http://www.tentmaker.org/Quotes/uniquotes.htm

[78] Kim Paffenroth. Judas: Images of the Lost Disciple. Westminster John Knox Press. Louisville, KY. 2001. 132.

[79] In the resurrection love is shown to be stronger than death Pope says at Easter Vigil. Catholic News Agency. 7 April 2007.

[80] The Basis of the Teaching of Universal Salvation. Destined For Salvation Ministries. 16 September 2012. http://www.destinedforsalvation.org/Basis.html

[81] Llewellyn Vaughan-Lee. Love is a Fire: The Sufi's Mystical Journey Home. The Golden Sufi Center. Inverness, CA. 2000. p. 124.

[82] Religious Diversity (Pluralism). Stanford Encyclopedia of Philosophy. 25 May 2004.

[83] Shinran Shonin. Project Gutenberg EBook of Buddhist Psalms. 2004.

[84] William Sutherland. Unum. Trafford Publishing. USA. 2012. pp. 303-304.

[85] Allen J. Christensen. Popol Vuh: Literal Translation. Mesoweb Publications. 29 November 2011. http://www.mesoweb.com/publications/Christensen/PV-Literal.pdf

William Sutherland

---

[86] Religious Diversity (Pluralism). Stanford Encyclopedia of Philosophy. 25 May 2004.

[87] What Does Judaism Say About Love? Moment. September/October 2010.

[88] Three Steps to Salvation. Connection. 2008. Issue 1. p. 14.

[89] Matthew Weinberg. The Human Rights Discourse: A Bahá'í Perspective. Bahá'í Topics. 15 July 2013. http://info.bahai.org/article-1-8-3-2.html

[90] Daniel Ladinsky. Love Poems from God: Twelve Sacred Voices from the East and West. Penguin. New York. 2002. p. 31.

[91] Three Steps to Salvation. Connection. 2008. Issue 1. p. 14.

[92] William Sutherland. Unum. Trafford Publishing. USA. 2012. p. 168.

[93] William Sutherland. Unum. Trafford Publishing. USA. 2012. p. 169.

[94] Universal Reconciliation. Wikipedia.org. 1 September 2012. http://en.wikipedia.org/wiki/Universal_reconciliation

[95] George Koehler. United Methodist Member's Handbook, Revised. 2006. pp. 77-78.

80

[96] Universal Reconciliation. Wikipedia.org. 1 September 2012. http://en.wikipedia.org/wiki/Universal_reconciliation

[97] Rabbi Brad Hirschfield. Celebrating Second Chances On Rosh HaShanah. The Jewish Week. 14 September 2012. p. 22.

[98] Three Steps to Salvation. Connection. 2008. Issue 1. p. 14.

[99] Sir John Templeton. Agape Love. Templeton Foundation Press. Philadelphia, PA. 1999. p. 39.

[100] Judaism vs. Christianity. 123.helpme.com. 15 September 2012. http://www.123helpme.com/view.asp?id=32783

[101] Universal Reconciliation. Wikipedia.org. 1 September 2012. http://en.wikipedia.org/wiki/Universal_reconciliation

[102] Llewellyn Vaughan-Lee. Love is a Fire: The Sufi's Mystical Journey Home. The Golden Sufi Center. Inverness, CA. 2000. p. 13.

[103] Daniel Ladinsky. Love Poems from God: Twelve Sacred Voices from the East and West. Penguin Compass. New York. 2002. p. 142.

[104] Tukaram. Can water drink itself? Poetry Chaikhana. 22 July 2013. http://www.poetry-chaikhana.com/T/Tukaram/Canwaterdrin.htm

[105] St. John of the Cross. The Living Flame of Love. BN.com. 22 July 2013. http://www.barnesandnoble.com/sample/read/2940014519953

William Sutherland

[106] Universalism of Salvation: St. Isaac The Syrian. 16 February 2012. http://www.crup.org/book/series04/IVA-32/chapter-7.htm

[107] Kim Paffenroth. Judas: Images of the Lost Disciple. Westminster John Knox Press. Louisville, KY. 2001. 142.

[108] Has the Pope been giving us to Hope that All will be Saved? Romancatholicism.org. 5 October 2012. http://www.romancatholicism.org/jpii-quotes.htm

[109] Universalism Through Church History... Quotes. Tentmaker.com. 3 October 2012. http://www.tentmaker.org/Quotes/uniquotes.htm

[110] James Weldon Johnson, ed. (1871–1938). The Book of American Negro Poetry. 1922. http://www.bartleby.com/269/30.html

[111] The Basis of the Teaching of Universal Salvation. Destined For Salvation Ministries. 16 September 2012. http://www.destinedforsalvation.org/Basis.html

[112] Llewellyn Vaughan-Lee. Love is a Fire: The Sufi's Mystical Journey Home. The Golden Sufi Center. Inverness, CA. 2000. p. 7.

[113] The Love of God. 19 September 2012. http://www.cyberhymnal.org/htm/l/o/loveofgo.htm

[114] Tony Lane. The Wrath of God as an Aspect of the Love of God. 2001. http://www.theologynetwork.org/doctrine-of-god/the-wrath-of-god-as-an-aspect-of-the-love-of-god.htm

[115] Tony Lane. The Wrath of God as an Aspect of the Love of God. 2001. http://www.theologynetwork.org/doctrine-of-god/the-wrath-of-god-as-an-aspect-of-the-love-of-god.htm

[116] Tony Lane. The Wrath of God as an Aspect of the Love of God. 2001. http://www.theologynetwork.org/doctrine-of-god/the-wrath-of-god-as-an-aspect-of-the-love-of-god.htm

[117] Dennis Ngien. The God who suffers. Christianity Today. 41.2. 3 February 1997.

[118] Sri Chinmoy. Love Human and Love Divine. Chinmoy.org. 27 February 1974. http://www.srichinmoy.org/resources/library/talks/philosophy/love_human_divine/index.html

[119] Esther Peperkamp. When God is Love: Reflections on Christian and Romantic Sentiments in Catholic Poland. Etnofoor. Vol. 19, No. 1. 2006. p. 96.

[120] Susan Sprecher and Beverley Fehr. Enhancement of Mood and Self-Esteem As A Result of Giving And Receiving Compassionate Love. Current Research In Social Psychology. Vol. 11, No. 16. 21 August 2006. pp. 229-230.

[121] Love. 16 September 2012. http://whitelilyoftrinity.com/saints_quotes_love.html

[122] Robert Roth. Choosing to love. Sojourners Magazine. 35.5. May 2006. p. 48.

[123] Sir John Templeton. Agape Love. Templeton Foundation Press. Philadelphia, PA. 1999. p. 15.

William Sutherland

[124] God Loves Us. Corpus Christi Parish.com. 16 September 2012.

[125] Daniel Ladinsky. Love Poems from God: Twelve Sacred Voices from the East and West. Penguin Compass. New York. 2002. pp. 302 and 309.

[126] God Loves Us. Corpus Christi Parish.com. 16 September 2012.

[127] Heaven and Hell According to Various Religions. 23 March 2007. http://www.neatorama.com/2007/03/23/heaven-and-hell-according-to-various-religions/

[128] Hell. Wikipedia.org. 15 September 2012. http://en.wikipedia.org/wiki/Hell

[129] Rabbi Max Weiman. Hell? No, we won't go. Kabbalah Made Easy.com. 17 September 2012. http://www.kabbalahmadeeasy.com/index.php?option=com_content&view=article&id=29:hell-no-we-wont-go&catid=14:basic-philosophy&Itemid=31

[130] Rabbi Max Weiman. Hell? No, we won't go. Kabbalah Made Easy.com. 17 September 2012. http://www.kabbalahmadeeasy.com/index.php?option=com_content&view=article&id=29:hell-no-we-wont-go&catid=14:basic-philosophy&Itemid=31

[131] Rob Bell. Love Wins. HarperOne. New York. 2011.

[132] Sun Myung Moon and Hyo Won Eu. Exposition of the Divine Principle. Sungwha Publishing Co., Seoul, South Korea. 2005.

[133] The Judgment of God: A Sufi Tale. Word Press.com. 17 September 2012. http://darvish.wordpress.com/2006/07/04/the-judgment-of-god-a-sufi-tale/

[134] Ben Coblentz. Born to Love. TGS International. Berlin, OH. 1993.

[135] William Sutherland. Unum. Trafford Publishing. USA. 2012. p. 332.

[136] Sir John Templeton. Agape Love. Templeton Foundation Press. Philadelphia, PA. 1999. pp. 25, 31.

[137] Jennifer O'Connor. I Love You. God's Love in Poetry. 23 July 2013. http://www.godsloveinpoetry.com/i-love-you.html

[138] God Loves Us. Corpus Christi Parish.com. 16 September 2012. http://www.corpuschristiparish.com/church/inspirational_quotes/255.pdf

[139] Martin Luther, "What to Look for and Expect in the Gospels." Martin Luther's Basic Theological Writings, Ed. Timothy F. Lull. 2nd Ed. Augsburg Fortress, Minneapolis, MN., 2005. p. 106.

[140] Quotes about God's Love. Goodreads. 16 July 2013. http://www.goodreads.com/quotes/tag/god-s-love

85

William Sutherland

[141] John Winthrop. A Modell of Christian Charity." 1630. http://www.academicamerican.com/colonial/docs/winthrop.htm

[142] Donagh O'Shea. The Madness of God. Goodnews.ie. 2009. http://www.goodnews.ie/jacobswellsdec.shtml

[143] Daniel Ladinsky. Love Poems from God: Twelve Sacred Voices from the East and West. Penguin Compass. New York. 2002. p. 41.

[144] God Loves Us. Corpus Christi Parish.com. 16 September 2012.

[145] Rev. Sun Myung Moon. The True Love Movement and the Unification Church. 18 September 2012. http://www.tparents.org/Moon-Books/bif1/BIF1-1-406.htm

[146] Daniel Ladinsky. Love Poems from God: Twelve Sacred Voices from the East and West. Penguin Compass. New York. 2002. p. 179.

[147] Whom Does God Love? The Christian Science Monitor. 28 July 1994.

[148] Daniel Ladinsky. Love Poems from God: Twelve Sacred Voices from the East and West. Penguin Compass. New York. 2002. p. 274.

[149] Roberta C. Bondi. Memories of God: a scholar discovers God where she did not want to look. Christianity Today. 39.8. 17 July 1995.

[150] Heaven's Truth Church: Sacred Book. 1998. http://heaventruth.com/sacred-book/

[151] Roberta C. Bondi. Memories of God: a scholar discovers God where she did not want to look. Christianity Today. 39.8. 17 July 1995.

[152] Deborah Ann Belka. Jesus Knows Your Pain. 3 December 2012. http://www.hiswingsshadow.com/

[153] Quote. The Christian's Den. 29 July 2013. http://thechristiansden.weebly.com/1/post/2013/07/quote136.html

[154] Roberta C. Bondi. Memories of God: a scholar discovers God where she did not want to look. Christianity Today. 39.8. 17 July 1995.

[155] Ronnie Miller. We Are Precious Stones In The Eyes of God. March 2009 Sermon. http://www.sermoncentral.com/sermons/we-are-precious-stones-in-the-eyes-of-god-ronnie-miller-sermon-on-atonement-159170.asp

[156] Dieter F. Uchtdorf. The Love of God. Church of Latter Day Saints. 21 February 2012. https://www.lds.org/general-conference/2009/10/the-love-of-god?lang=eng

[157] Margaret Murney Glenn. Christian Science: The Revelation of Love as Divine Principle. 1 December 1933. http://www.cslectures.org/Glenn/CS-The%20Revelation%20of%20Love-Glenn.htm

[158] The Philosophy of Divine Love. 17 July 2013. http://www.divine-innocence.org/Philosophy%20of%20Divine%20Love.htm

[159] The Philosophy of Divine Love. 17 July 2013.
http://www.divine-
innocence.org/Philosophy%20of%20Divine%20Love.htm

[160] Roberta C. Bondi. Memories of God: a scholar discovers
God where she did not want to look. Christianity Today. 39.8.
17 July 1995.

[161] Rachel Held Evans. Let love win in me. 28 July 2013.
http://rachelheldevans.com/blog/love-wins-in-me

[162] William Sutherland. Unum. Trafford Publishing. USA.
2012. p. 149.

William Sutherland

Epilogue: Poetry and Haiku

As a reflection and confirmation of God's everlasting *agape* love, I conclude with poetry and haiku that I hope are comforting, thought provocative and will leave a lasting impression that can serve as a catalyst to spark a greater love that is unbiased and impulsively and freely given to all regardless of one's individuality and cultural, racial, gender, age, genetic differences and disability (if applicable) so that it comes a fraction closer to that of God.

It is also my hope that the below poetry and haiku can usher in ecumenical unity and interfaith cooperation through diversity and respect and help build a stronger, lasting and ultimate permanent peace between peoples, religions, and nations.

The Aftermath
Dedicated to every victim of war, genocide, persecution, and torture

Cities lie in ruin, families in shambles,
Cold and hunger pervade, death and disease
dominate.
Uncertainty and helplessness prevail – What have
we done? Why have we turned away from God's
love?

Though tears of sorrow have all been spent
And the weeping has ceased, painful memories

90

linger in hearts that ache in melancholy mourning.
What have we done?
Was the desire to rule, possess and conquer worth
turning away from God's love?

Voices have fallen silent, faces are but mere
memories;
The little comforts of life once taken for granted
Are nowhere to be found.
Joy and happiness are vestiges of the past,
Spirits sag with gloom and doubt.
Mounds of disheveled dirt fill once verdant
pastures,
Drab markers declare the tragic toll in lives;
What have we done? Was the price in lost lives
worth turning away from God's love?

Bonds of trust lie shattered and broken
Friendships twisted and mangled,
Communities splintered and dispersed;
All suffer victim to injustice and hatred,
All are prisoner to despair
Exiled among the indiscriminant destruction –
Innocent, unwilling victims to great ineffable evil.
What have we done? Was it worth turning away
from God's love?

The once living fill mass graves,
The still living are forever scarred,
The air that reeks of rotting flesh,
The stains of blood that color everything around

91

Testify to the annihilated sanctity of life.
What have we done? Was it worth turning away
from God's love?

Can anything be worth such a steep price?
How long before time heals, if ever?
How much pain do we have to inflict?
How much more do we have to endure?
When will we finally learn?
How long before we embrace God's *agape* love?

Beauty

Beauty comes in the most complex and simplest of
forms –
Seen only by eyes whose view is clear and
unclouded,
Heard by ears open to all
And recognized by minds free of prejudice.

Without its mix of shades, complexions and colors
It would be bland and unseen;
Deprived of its varied sounds, symbols and words
It would be dull and unheard;
Without its individuality and blend of culture and
customs
It would be unnoticed and unappreciated.

Though sights everywhere lure the eyes
And sounds of musical harmony entice the ears –
True beauty lives and breathes all around us

Encapsulated in heterogeneous bodies
Sculpted in the Image of God.

True beauty lies in peoples of all lands, color,
gender and culture –
The intertwined threads that comprise God's
mosaic of love.

The Children of War

Dedicated to the Children of Čapljina (Bosnia-Herzegovina) whom I
had met in 1993 during the Bosnian War before they were subseqently
and senselessly massacred.

The Children of War are like little flowers trampled,
Young and innocent, fragile and helpless;
Surrounded by violence and rampant destruction –
Their tiny faces filled with doubts and fear.

The Children of War, so precious and dear,
Stripped of their childhood years – with their youth
Stolen away are little saints
For human failing through no fault or choice of their
own.

The Children of War, their lives lost and scarred
Are the world's hopes and future wasted;
They are the cures never found, inventions never
made, dreams unfulfilled, thoughts and ideas
forever gone – An irrational tragedy with no
justification to be found.
The Children of War are the victims of
Our grievous failure to heed God's great command

93

To love thy neighbor as thyself –
And a reflection of our greatest affront to His all-
embracing love.

Dawn

Each dawn, greeted by growing brightness
Brings a new day filled with expectation and hope.

Each dawn, the manifestation of God's *agape* love
Is a renewal of time and a chance for new
beginnings.

The Easter Lily

The Easter lily is a delicate, humble flower of God,
Simple, incorrupt and pure – Of infinite worth
With resplendent beauty free of imperfection,
blemish and stain.

The Easter lily, in total surrender
Lovingly serves the will of God without as much
As a resisting whimper or whine.

The Easter lily with its immaculate impeccable
figure
Is a heavenly font flowing with sanctified serenity –
A symbol of resurrection and eternity.

The Easter lily with its angelic white petals
Stands as an unwavering witness to
The *agape* love of God.

94

The Easter lily with its pristine, joyful form
Offers a tiny glimpse of the Kingdom
That awaits us all.

Ecstasy

Sitting in prayerful reflection,
Filled with an indescribable tranquil joy,
One cannot help but feel God's palpable
Unconditional love.

With mind free of conscious awareness
And body liberated from earthly burdens,
If but for only a fleeting moment,
The heart leaps joyfully heavenward.

Though mere words cannot even begin to describe
The mystical experience our Lord provides –
without our even asking,
It is a sure taste of the Heavenly Kingdom's
Imperishable fruits of blissful love to come.

The Eternal Flame

The Eternal Flame
Quietly flickers in remembrance of victims past –
Lost so tragically to war, genocide and the other
iniquities of our human failings.

Reflecting long and hard in somber silence,
All the while staring into the mournful flame,

Watching the placid wisps of drifting smoke,
One can vaguely visualize the indelible doleful sea
of faces
And faintly hear the imperceptible whispers of the
Countless martyred innocents of so many ages
past.

The Eternal Flame is
Our burning testament of remorse and contrition,
An enduring reminder of our past failings,
The perpetual upholding of our promise to never
forget,
And a radiant symbol of our hopes and dreams
For a brighter and better future of lasting justice
and peace.

The Eternal Flame is a burning inspiration –
If we learn from our mistakes
And strive to accept and spread
God's *agape* love among us
We can truly have the utopic world
He so desires.

God's Wondrous Love

God's wondrous love is infinite and limitless
Such that He gave of Himself
A Savior to save us all!

God's wondrous love is an all-encompassing font of
mercy such that all are cleansed, purified and

saved.

God's wondrous love is so ineffably great that
A sinner today can be a saint tomorrow!

God's wondrous love is so expansive and wide
One should never despair of hope
For there is a place in His Glorious Kingdom for all!

God's wondrous love is so ineffably great –
He never forsakes a single being of His making!

Humanity

We are many Peoples,
Though male and female and young and old
Of many races and cultures and tongues and
beliefs,
Each endowed with our own unique individuality –
We are all of the same species born in the image of
God.

We are many Peoples
Though divided by human-made lines and borders,
Institutions and beliefs, language and customs
And symbols and words,
We are of the same world, blessed with the same
free will,
Worthy of the same dignified respect
All because we have been given purpose and worth
by the Divine Creator.

97

We are many Peoples
Each with an inimitable, indelible face
That constitutes an essential tiny drop in the
ever changing renewed waters that comprise the
vast sea of humanity.

We are many Peoples
Called to live in peace and harmony –
For an assault on any of us by another
Through hatred, anti-Semitism, racism and
discrimination is an affront to
God's divine plan,
An insult to His infinite wisdom and
A desecration of the ineffable beauty of His human
creation.

Life

Life is like a burning candle,
The flame the soul, the candle the body.

Brightly it burns
Glowing with vibrance;
Tranquil and controlled,
Fragile and mortal,
Yet potent in anger.
Sometimes slowly, sometimes quickly it burns,
Leaving its tiny indelible mark.

With the passing of time,
The candle melts, the flame dims

And with a flicker,
Silently passes with a puff of smoke
On its invisible journey –
Only possible because of God's enduring *agape*
love.

Mercy

Mercy is the manifestation of God's great love.
It is our chance to start anew each time
We stumble and fall.

Mercy is the love that forgives
For God knows our every weakness and flaw.

Mercy is the love that saves
For through works alone we'd be hopelessly lost.

Mercy is the love that is God
For God is love and love is mercy.

New Dawn

Every new dawn brings greater courage and hope
To succeed where only yesterday we had stumbled
and fallen.

Every new dawn offers spiritual renewal –
For God's loving mercy is boundless and unending.

Every new dawn offers spiritual inspiration
As we carry our precious little cross towards

99

heavenly eternity.

Every new dawn brings ever greater joy
As we draw closer to our loving Creator.

Our Loving Saving God

Who can be so good as to love as He could only
do?

Who can be so great that He dwells among the
lowly and the meek?

Who could be so rich that He feeds the hungry and
the poor?

Who could be so kind that He soothes and heals
the lonely and the sick?

Who could be so tolerant and open that He
embraces the rejected and the condemned?

Who could be of such infinite love that He gives the
breath of life to us mere children of dust?

Who could be of such selfless love that He
humbled His divinity to the lowly state of our human
flesh?

Who could be of such great love that He offered
Himself as the sacrificial lamb?

Who could be of such awesome love that He saves

us all but our loving saving God!

The Springtime Dawn

A menagerie of colors – ocher, amber, orange and
red
Tint the horizon's wispy clouds;
Streaming rays of light bursting from the rising sun
above
Chase the thick nocturnal darkness,
Basking the earth in soothing, ambient warmth.

Creatures dormant stir to life,
Sleep's stasis gradually ebbs away;
A new morning dawns – A fresh beginning
Filled with much potential, promise and hope.

A misty morning dew clothes all the plants around,
Drops of moisture trickle to the earthen ground,
Refreshing vegetation everywhere around.

Pockets of fog shroud rolling hills and
Verdant country pastures alike,
A placid breeze softly caresses April's
Panoramic flowery blossoms,
Enveloping the waking morning world
In an atmosphere of undisturbed blissful solitude.

The nascent day's gentle warmth,
Absorbed by all and everything around,
Casts the earth under an ineffable wondrous spell –

101

The springtime dawn is surely the essence of the
Renewal of Life – A tiny hint of the
Resurrection's power of love.

Total Surrender

Without total surrender to the will of God,
In body, mind and soul
You will never truly know the depth of His *agape*
love.

If you fully surrender yourself to God,
You will appreciate His gifts and graces,
And never be in want or need.

If you surrender yourself to the will of God,
You will joyfully carry your little cross,
All the while,
Showering Him with thanks, prayers and praise.

And if you fully surrender yourself to God,
You will discover and appreciate –
Your faith is the greatest gift of all.

The Unsung Plant

In the wintry cold, a tiny seed planted by the
Invisible Hand of God, peacefully sleeps,
Safely tucked beneath the ground,
Blanketed by frosted sheets of silvery-white.

With the arrival of the springtime thaw,

A tiny plant awaiting its day
Bursts from the safety of its seed,
Awakened by warmth and gentle showers of rain.

Guided by an abundance of hope and an
unquenchable zest for life,
The tiny plant, ever the optimist
Conquers impediments large and small.

Firmly staking its delicate roots deep within the
ground,
Its stem springs from the earth
Reaching for the azure heavens above.

Like the rejected,
Though unjustly stripped of its worth – unfairly
labeled a weed,
The unsung plant makes the most of its uncertain
and difficult life,
Giving to nature's spectrum of colors and varied
collection of scents.

Though its tiny indelible gift – beauty in the purest
and simplest form
Goes unnoticed by unappreciating myopic eyes,
God's great love cherishes and adores its very
being!

Water

Cool and refreshing,

Cleansing and healing,
Clear and colorless,
Tangible and wet,
A mirror of shapes and designs,
A prism of shades and colors,
Everywhere, all around,
In the air, in the clouds,
In the rain, in the ground,
In rivers and streams, and oceans and lakes,
In plants and animals and all that breathe – the
essence of God's omnipresent love.

More abundant than gold and silver,
And all the riches of the world,
Yet much more precious – the substance of life
Emblematic of God's infinite selfless love!

Unceasing and flowing,
So simple and pure,
The eternal reflection of God's outpouring
indiscriminate love!

The Will of God

Let the will of God be done,
Let Him do unto me as He wills,
For through my joyful adversities,
I know not to fear – for God is Love
And Love heals and mends,
Guides and serves
And forgives and saves.

Haiku 俳句 :

Good Friday's great love,
Jesus nailed to the cross –
Salvation for all!

Divine Royalty
Crowned in thorns, clothed in purple –
God's love on the cross.

God's love never fails
It is unbiased and free
The cross stands as proof.

Personal success
Does not matter to heaven –
Christ's victory does!

No one is to blame
God laid down His life through love
To save all the world.

Painful thorns still pierce
The God of love – Nature sheds
Tiny drops of dew.

Without divine love
The grave would hold us captive
Yet death has no sting!

105

William Sutherland

How great is God's love?
It loved you into being
And gave salvation!

God touched nothingness
And so began the saga
of unending love!

Without Divine breath,
I would be but lifeless dust –
God's love gives me life.

God is perfect love –
He gives us new beginnings
Each passing second!

A new dawn beckons,
Light and warmth chase dark and cold –
God's love hugs the soul.

Everyone God makes
He cherishes above all
Through eternal love!

So great is God's love,
There is a place in His heart
Including for me!

God embraces all,
His awesome love knows no bounds,
Your name completes Him.

The heart of God's love
Is a clasped double heart –
His heart joined with yours!

The heart of God's love
Is open like none other –
It beats, "I love you!"

The sole hope I need
Is knowledge that God is love –
His love heals and saves.

Just call Him "Abba" –
Though God goes by many names,
We are His children.

Out of divine love
We are heirs to the Kingdom
God's sons and daughters.

When I am alone
Feeling hurt and abandoned
God's love is with me!

The sun and the moon –
Luminescent comforters
Show God's love for all.

Though so clear and bright,
Each pixel will dim and fade;
God's love will endure!

William Sutherland

Like an iPad's screen
That responds to every touch,
God answers prayer.

Our genetic code,
The software of our being
Is God's script of love!

As the Internet
Is seen by distant peoples,
God sees all our needs.

Spring showers and warmth
Bring brightness, colors and life –
God's love among us.

Whispers in the ears,
Imperceptible advice –
God's loving guidance.

Though often ignored
And rejected by many –
God's love never stops!

To know God's great love,
One need not be a scholar –
One just needs to be!

Before you were born,
I loved you – Though I know all,
I love you still more!

The image God sees
When looking in a mirror
Is pitiful me.

God's loving heart melts
On seeing pitiful me –
It hugs and comforts.

Free of suffering,
Filled with exquisite beauty
Is heaven to come.

Enraptured by bliss
Forever embraced by love
Is life eternal!

God is inclusive
Such that salvation includes
Plants and animals.

Life is a journey –
A chance to perfect our love
As God so desires.

Let all humankind
Forsake judgment of others
And open their hearts.

Let all humankind
Foresake the weapons of war
And take up kind acts.

109

Hidden from the eyes,
True beauty flows from within,
Seen only by God.

Most rich mosaic
Covering lands near and far –
World humanity.

Though we can't see Him,
God is present among us
In all living things.

Most precious jewels,
Tiny gems of divine love –
Every little child.

Let all religions
Be a light unto nations
And proclaim God's love!

Ancient Jewish Oil Lamp

With oil for one day,
The Chanukkah lamp burned eight –
Miracle of love.

110

From the beginning,
God had a beautiful plan –
Let love prevail!

Let all religions
Embrace all God's creation
Through loving guidance.

Like pearls in the sea,
Nuggets of God's love are found
In each religion.

They hid in Eden,
And humankind seemed hopeless –
God's love persevered!

Insurmountable
As it may seem to appear –
God's love is able!

Like falling snowflakes
Make a winter wonderland –
God transforms the soul.

Looking at a pond
Teeming with all sorts of life –
Eden of God's love.

Whispering cattails
Wafting in the gentle breeze –
God's voice among us.

William Sutherland

In scary darkness
Filled with peril and danger,
God's love lights the way!

Fallen autumn leaves
A colorful mosaic –
A glimpse of God's love.

The starry night sky,
Bright speckles in the darkness,
Lamps to guide the soul.

Drops of rain and dew,
Heaven's baptismal waters
Renew all around.

The changing seasons
Symbolize our life's phases –
God's love is constant.

Like a bonsai tree
One needs a small amount faith
To know divine love.

Absent little faith
One does not know divine love –
But it still loves you!